America, Can She Be Fixed?

by

Michael Alan Kaiser

DORRANCE PUBLISHING CO., INC.
PITTSBURGH, PENNSYLVANIA 15222

ISBN: 978-1-4349-0485-0
Library of Congress Control Number: 2008938946

Printed in the United States of America

First Printing

For information or to order additional books, please write:
Dorrance Publishing Co., Inc.
701 Smithfield St.
Pittsburgh, Pennsylvania 15222
U.S.A.
1-800-788-7654
www.dorrancebookstore.com

Prologue

As I sit down to write this, I am still in the middle of writing a book on beer and beer-related travel—things I am most certainly an expert on. I will have to get back to chapter six of that novel someday soon. However, I have taken a break to write this book. It may never get published, or even be given a second look. Still, I feel it is important to cut through some of the political BS and red tape, and start taking responsibility and accountability for our actions before it is too late. In fact, it may already be too late. I certainly hope that is not the case. I will pull no punches, pointing the finger at some people by name, some not, but you all know who you are. The people responsible for bringing the greatest country on Earth to the brink of collapse—and you definitely know who you are—simply must pay the fiddler.

We will discuss what must be repaired, how to repair it, and perhaps how to avoid such disasters in the future. I am very concerned about my children's future in this country. So much so, I have seriously contemplated moving back to Germany. We need to stop taking such bad advice from people who could not find their butts with a map and a pack of search dogs. Use your common sense; trust your own instincts, upbringing, and experiences; and, if it sounds too good to be true, always remember that it most likely is so. Most importantly, we must stop finger-pointing, passing the buck, and wasting time and energy on things that are far from the truth. Let's stand up and start taking responsibility for our own actions as Americans.

I will not pull any punches, or worry about hurting anyone's feelings. It is time to stop treading softly so we do not offend a specific group, race, gender, religion, or party. This once great country still has the potential to be great, and our diversity and variety make it so. With that being said, we cannot spend too much time being politically correct over the next ten years. Let's all get on the same page and repair what is broken. We need to fix America now; then worry about what may be happening thousands of miles away. A handful of greedy, self-serving, unsupervised crooks have rocked the nation and world to their very cores financially and otherwise. Let us get started on a solution without pointing fingers, laying blame, and handing out punishment until after we get things back on track.

Chapter 1
Not Nearly As Good As We Think

How the mighty have fallen. The state of affairs in a once great nation has become disgustingly pathetic on many levels. When traveling abroad, I no longer have the answers. I cannot explain how the mighty United States of America has become a laughing stock in conversations around the world. This book will not be pretty, patriotic, or flattering in any way. Many years of failure at the leadership level in America have brought me to this point. I am certainly a "glass is half-full," optimistic person about my own life. In fact, I have been that way about almost everything for as far back as I can remember. The very foundation of what was once the model for democracy has crumbled. In my humble opinion, it has done so from the top down. Many disturbing facts will back this up. I am not going to cut and paste a ton of news clips from either the liberal or extreme right media. I will not quote a myriad of statistics to show how far we have fallen, as we have all seen it with our own eyes. Common sense is a term either applied or uttered enough in today's America, and that truly is a shame. Our leaders in politics, business, education, law, and finance have failed us miserably. This is indeed a crisis that could have been avoided had we applied common sense to most situations.

Moreover, our "cream of the crop" leaders in Washington and on Wall Street have showed no backbone in the past thirty years or more. Nobody wants to take responsibility, despite being able to see the mortgage crisis, stock market failure, federal deficit, health care issues, and immigration issues, just to name a few, coming straight at us full speed.

I am almost as guilty as anyone else. I have become fat and lazy myself, a product of my unmotivated environment, despite knowing what I need to do to make myself a better man. Where do we point the finger? Is it the technological and computer age? Is it the internet? Let us not kid ourselves on this issue. The Western world is still run by human beings. Those human beings have to be held accountable for the massive failures at almost every critical level, but none of these individuals have raised his hand to admit fault or guilt. In recent years, we have prosecuted a few folks, making scapegoats of a few rich guys and gals. However, the Kenneth Lays, Martha Stewarts, Bernie Ebbers, Scott Sullivans, Dennis Kozloskis, and Lehman Brothers of the world are certainly not alone in this moral breakdown of the US corporate-financial system.

Can we blame the educational system for such failures? Think about it for a moment. If our CEOs, COOs, and presidents of once large and mighty corporations with thousands of employees and billions in assets are incompetent, what chance do we have of running my own small businesses? At some point it appears to have become not only acceptable, but quite normal to inflate the company stock as much as humanly possible, even if that means lying through your teeth about almost everything. That is a really scary and disturbing way to run things. We have become a society of smoke and mirrors.

How deep does this failure in the corporate financial world go? Has this been going on for twenty-five years, fifty years, perhaps since the day the US Stock Exchange was born? Recent events and disclosures about corporate balance sheets have revealed that our business leaders have not only been using way too much credit to "grow" their respective companies and corporations, but have not been using "real" cash at all. Our unrealistic spend, spend, spend-till-you-cannot-spend-anymore attitude has literally written a trillion-dollar balance that we will never be able to collect on. Not in my lifetime anyway. Wall Street alone is not to blame. In the modern era, one word has absolutely destroyed the fabric of our once proud country. That word is greed. This word has always been man's downfall, but we have taken it to new heights during my forty-three years years on the planet.

Can we blame the glitz and glamour of Hollywood? We have been watching the big screen and television stars for over fifty years now, hoping, wishing, and praying that we could live in a fantasy world like our celebrity heroes. So many people have been so busy trying to be something they are not, trying so hard to impress complete strangers, we have forgotten who we really are inside. We have spent entirely too much energy in our lifetimes, pretending to have more material things than our neighbors. The yuppie lifestyle is indeed a microcosm of the American corporate way of doing things. We mistakenly think that driving a fancy, expensive, foreign car will make us a better person—even if that means going eighty thousand dollars in debt, making payments for eight years to the bank on said automobile. If you drive back and forth to work five or six days per week, and the car sits in the parking lot, does it matter if it costs twenty thousand or eighty thousand dollars in reality?

How many Americans are spending 60 percent of two full-time incomes on a mortgage they truly cannot afford? It should be common sense to not pay over one third of your income on rent or mortgage payments. If you own a home in an upper–middle-class neighborhood and you have to put all the furniture, landscaping, and extras on credit cards, is this smart? Not only is it not smart, this kind of thing is digging a financial grave that many of us will never be able to get out of. The number of Americans with a thirty-year mortgage and owing over half a million dollars in interest over the term of the loan to the bank is staggering. Many of these same people owe another one hundred thousand dollars on auto loans and credit cards with even more interest. It seems that in both the corporate and private sectors, we write checks our butts cannot cash instead of staying within our means. Once again, just applying common sense would serve us greatly on such matters. We choose not to do so. This kind of thing has served as a very poor example for our youth in America for so many years, generations simply do not know any better. We have become fat, drunk, lazy, and downright stupid. I know, because I am right there with most of you.

Over the past twenty years, I have traveled to Germany and Austria once or twice per year. I find it interesting to see firsthand how the attitude towards the United States has changed so drastically during this time frame. As recently as the late 1980s, many Germans and other Europeans viewed Americans as successful, strong, rich, and perhaps even a bit cocky. This has changed so much in recent years. In fact, since 2001 or so, we have become a laughing stock in the eyes of millions and millions of others around the globe. I always get questions like, "Why do so many Americans get married when they do not know anything about one another?" I tell them it is because there are no consequences for our actions. Even those of us who are supposedly educated, well bred, and experienced in many ways tend to make absolutely mind-bogglingly silly decisions. The worldwide web has certainly not helped us. Getting your face on YouTube or some other website is not only easy, but very inexpensive these days. From the outside looking inward, we are simply morons, making the same mistakes over and over again. This does not bother most Americans, as they mistakenly see the rest of the world as insignificant, distant, and unimportant.

Greed is not the only deadly sin we have used to fail on such a massive level. Technically, the term "selfishness" is not on the famed list of seven deadly sins. In my opinion, the list should be altered to include this word. I believe this personality trait has been the root cause of so many family, personal, romantic, financial, and moral disasters, we almost seem to enjoy beating ourselves up this way. Each and every day, when just doing something simple like driving to work, we see it. People so wrapped up in their own little world, chatting on the cell phone about nothing, they nearly run someone off the road, or run over a small child, never knowing how close they came to changing the lives of so many people. We do not think of our fellow man and woman enough, putting ourselves first in almost every scenario. Americans love to idolize others. It has always fascinated us to look up to celebs, sports heroes, etc. Still, we see these very people failing at life each and every day. There is no common-sense checklist applying to marriage, raising children, community, financial responsibility, or setting a good example for our young folks. We selfishly continue to make the same silly mistakes over and over and over again. In this day and age, spoiled-rotten, selfish morons can stop at a drive-thru wedding chapel in Las Vegas, get their drunk asses married at 2:00 AM, then laugh about it. Six weeks later, they are in front of a judge, getting a quick divorce.

Do not even get me started on our court systems here in the US. Wow! What a complete and utter mess! Well, okay, I do have something to say on the matter. Along with the massive, hugely disappointing failures on Wall Street and the business world, this is the other area in which we have failed on a catastrophic level. The United States of America was once the model for judicial systems around the world. Now, we are held together with toothpicks and a small amount of cheap glue. Once again, in most cases for purely selfish reasons, we tie up the court systems with completely frivolous and ridiculous lawsuits on a daily basis, and it has become a very serious matter. This sickens me, as it does many hard-working folks. I hate to beat a dead horse but where in the hell is the common sense? This is another matter in which I can point to obvious breakdowns in the system without pointing to specific stats, charts, polls, etc. In my mind, those things are just like our financial system and stock market: twisted and skewed to say what the powers-that-be want them to say. Statistics are no longer based on fact, but speculation, lies, and completely unrealistic balance sheets.

So, I choose to point the finger at what we can clearly see with own collective eyes. There are too many frivolous lawsuits, too many lawyers, and too many lazy Americans suing for no reason whatsoever. Well, that is not entirely true. These people want something for nothing. There are fifteen thousand attorneys in the yellow pages. *Surely, one of these lawyers can get me some money 'cause so and so called me a name, right? Certainly, I am entitled to a few million because my klutzy ass fell on the sidewalk in front of the hardware store—am I correct?* It was not my fault at all. This is how we think in today's lazy, selfish, get-a-quick-dollar-without-working-for-it society. Grown men and women with university educations get married after three months of sleeping together; have children; then figure out they have nothing in common, did not really know each another, and have serious differences in their core-belief systems. Good thing you figured that out after having a few children, because they will be better off when you split the family up. These situations can be avoided if we use common sense and plan for what are supposed to be our most important life decisions. Even though we know this to be true, we ignore the signs, and jump off the bridge head first anyway. Do we really need to spend one hundred and fifty dollars per hour for some overopinionated buffoon in Southern California to tell us that we are dysfunctional, stressed, and selfish? Not at all, because we would know it all too well if we simply opened our collective eyes for a moment.

The masses in America continually make poor choices in life, love, education, career, and health matters. Wake up, people! These are very important decisions that will define us as human beings. Let us take a look at the number of divorce attorneys, malpractice attorneys, and personal injury attorneys...the list goes on and on. It's not acceptable to say "We are human and we make many mistakes" when we learn nothing from them. How many times must we self-destruct before we start doing things correctly? America is perhaps the country in the world in which what amounts to fix-what-we-knew-not–to-break-in-the-first-place industries thrive to the tune of billions and billions of dollars each year. We have become a truly dysfunctional society, ruled by the almighty dollar, greed, lust, envy, and selfishness. Sound familiar? Do I really need to point this out? Do many of us not already know this stuff, perhaps deep down? If it were so obvious, and did not need to be said, we would have surely done something to fix things from the top down by now. Therefore, I have to say something. We all must face the fact that we as a nation have become broken.

Only in America do we see a five-foot-three, one-hundred-and-ten-pound female driving a small school bus disguised as an Escalade, Suburban, or Ford Excursion. Driving such a vehicle down the freeway twenty miles per hour over the limit, talking to her sister or friends about absolutely nothing of substance on the cell phone is a recipe for disaster. Moreover, it's embarrassing. I think we need to take a look at our collective selves from an outside view. We badly need to take a look at America from afar in order to appreciate just how selfish and stupid and lazy we have really become. How many millionaires do we have in Southern California? Now, how many of them have made their millions as a direct result of taking advantage of dysfunctional people? It is a disgustingly obvious thing, but we tend to look the other way, and say, "Well, that's just the way it is these days" in most cases. These millionaires take advantage of people at their lowest point, sucking them dry not only financially, but emotionally in many cases, without ever curing them. Yes, I am talking about the huge industry of psychiatric care. How broken have we become when there are more shrinks, ambulance chasers, plastic surgeons, and fraud attorneys in each and every city than there are teachers, scientists, and community leaders? Answer: We are completely broken.

On the issue of the US judicial system, now that I am on a tangent here: Where did it go wrong? When did the system become a personal wealth tool for crooks, criminals, lazy do-nothing-and-collect-a-check fake people? It most likely started long before my birth in 1965, but certainly has gotten way out of proportion in the past forty or so years. Think about the root problem for a moment. Ask yourself how many lawyers were in each medium-to-large city per one thousand cities citizens in 1950, then compare it to that same number of folks in 2008. Without even looking at the actual numbers, I am certain it is quite alarming. This also creates another problem: one obvious to me, but perhaps not so for most. We have lowered our standards quite drastically. Before my time, becoming a lawyer was a very difficult thing to do. There were only a handful of prestigious, acclaimed, well respected institutions offering law degrees, and only the best of the best could qualify, much less graduate. That is simply no longer the case. Men and women of completely average intelligence are able to secure a law degree, and pass the Bar exam after a few attempts these days. The system pushes them through, and bends the learning curve to suit itself, because of our overall laziness, greed, and personal abuse of a once-great system of law. One of the things we need very badly in this country is an all-or-nothing or winner-take-all system. The American way of law allows for people to sue for no reason, without the risk of losing. Attorneys will take almost any case for a few bucks up front, no matter how ridiculous, based on historical percentages, and guarantee no additional fees—unless you win the case. Let me tell you something: This is the only place on earth where a person has a chance in hell of winning 75 percent of these cases. Thousands of embarrassingly silly lawsuits would be dismissed before they got to the docket if we had a backbone. If the system was not based entirely on money and a silly thing like protecting the citizens (insert sarcasm here), the average big city circuit court judge would not have a stack of cases ceiling-high each and every day of the week.

Suing one another for such things as "slander" and tying up the courts with one unnecessary divorce case after another is merely the tip of the iceberg. Let's face it, people: Some of you are too selfish, insecure, childish, and down-right stupid to run your own lives. With that in mind, remember that getting married and having children is not a very good plan. Get your act together on a personal, self-accountable level before you become a burden on the lives of so many others. We are much too quick to throw a few hundred dollars at a complete stranger, who then tells us our child has ADHD or some other made-up-for-money BS spoon fed to us by the medical industry. The vast majority of these issues could be fixed in the home, without too much effort, if we simply applied common sense and a bit of passion. Like the recently failed Wall Street fat cats on everyone's mind, we tend to point the finger at anyone but ourselves, never accepting responsibility for failing on any level. No backbone to be seen. The average American has two hundred channels on his or her cable TV or satellite system, with almost nothing worth watching at any given moment. Is it any wonder we are getting dumber by the year? We use hundreds of programs based on nothing more than opinion as our education, instead of reading factual books. The folks at MSN, CNN, Fox News, and several others know exactly what I am talking about. In fact, they count on it.

Another clear-cut example of our brains taking a virtual beating with a stupid stick on a daily basis is the popular "reality" TV garbage. I cannot figure this one out completely. Even when the producers in Hollywood and New York come up with a slightly interesting, almost worthwhile theme for such a show, the people have zero personality, zero intelligence, zero talent of any kind. These kind of shows truly redefine the term "waste of time." One would literally benefit more from going outside and watching the grass grow. Reality TV was created for two reasons and two reasons only. Firstly, the creative folks have run out of ideas. Secondly, the networks need to keep their cash flows flowing, so they have to fill the aforementioned 200 channels with junk 24/7/365. And that is just what 90 percent of television has become. To say reality TV is uninteresting, mind numbing, and really idiotic is a huge understatement.

Americans have become just as easily amused at the box office. How many times can we see the same shoot-'em-up-and-blow-shit-up-in-the-same-manner crap at the theater? This again is the direct result of Hollywood needing to keep cash flowing, and their being able to count on mindless American sheep flocking to the theaters to see the same thing over and over. Almost every once-original idea has been done to death, so the producers and directors just keep regurgitating 1970s television characters and remaking the same movie three or four times. As long as you space it out a few years, get a guy with a really deep voice to hype it on the trailer, and blow things up, people will not hesitate to spend nine dollars on it. Hollywood bimbos with store-bought boobs and lips do not have to have talent any longer. They just have to look good in tights, skimpy outfits. I am not an old fogie, and I have enough sense to know all too well that sex sells. However, make it interesting for us at least. A girl with large, fake breasts, tons of makeup, oil all over her skin, and perfect lighting cannot make her a good singer-songwriter. Let's come up with an original idea that everyone can appreciate before we ask for another twenty million.

The music industry is perhaps even worse than the motion picture industry, and that is really saying something. I will touch on each of the aforementioned issues, and several more. Just bitching about these things does almost no good. What we need are answers, fixes, solutions, and solid advice from people who actually apply common sense to almost everything they do. Opinions are all we see and hear these days, so I will do my best to do a bit more than talk and ramble on about change. Perhaps I can provide a solution or two. We keep regurgitating the same crap over and over again and expect to make even more money than the original version did.

Chapter 2
Marriage No Longer Sacred

A once holy, sacred, and respected bond has become a mockery in America. We have taken marriage and turned it into an absolute circus. There was a time when the families of two young people in love got together with a future plan, financial plan, housing plan, educational plan, etc. They would do whatever it took to ensure these two young people were not only right for one another, but would not become a burden on the families, the church, and the community. We tend to view marriage as a very simple choice with no consequences, no real counseling, not even a blood test any more. Simply head to the drive thru in Vegas, or even get married in fifteen minutes by Elvis in the back of a Cadillac. So many marriages are doomed for failure before they even start. We know this, but go forward with marriage for silly reasons like sexual chemistry, financial convenience, avoiding or sharing child support from previous marriages, etc. Many Americans take marriage so lightly, they stress more about a car loan or credit card payment than they do about choosing the person they are not only going to live with, but could spend the rest of their natural lives with. Making sure we know one another very, very well before jumping in to a bond like marriage is just not high on our list of priorities these days.

So many problems are created because we have made it so easy and convenient to get hitched, it's almost as if we are doing this on purpose, so that income can be generated for divorce lawyers, shrinks, and child support agencies. We have simply become a nation of "Let's see how it goes" people, jumping in to bad relationships headfirst, hoping it won't fall apart in six months. How can we be this bad at marriage? How can we look at a 55 percent to 60 percent national divorce rate as anything less than a completely embarrassing failure? Marriage should not only be a sacred bond between a man and a woman, but should be something that takes place between two people with some level of common sense, maturity, and self respect. Instead, people simply jump in and out of bed with whomever, contract an STD, and get pregnant, then say to each other, "Hey, let's get married and split the rent in our apartment or double-wide trailer for a spell." Whatever happened to getting your college degree, planning where you want to live for the long term, actually getting to know each another while courting, then saving money for a home and family? These things should be very basic rules to live by, or you will face dooming yourselves to fail quickly, creating animosity between each another for many years to come. More importantly, this kind of lackadaisical attitude towards the foundation of marriage makes things very difficult when we break up the home for the children involved. This is all unavoidable in my opinion.

We can fix this kind of thing in many instances, long before it becomes a broken mess. Firstly, do not move in with, or wed, a stranger. Ladies, if you meet a guy in a bar, the sex is good for three weeks, and he drives a nice car, this is not a sign that he is "the one" and your soul mate. We should have more sense than that. Learn about each another over time, giving yourself ample opportunities to see if you can deal with stress together. It is extremely important to find out of your lover is a responsible person. Does he or she pay the bills, have a good education, tell the truth about everything, and have a possessive nature? Simple common sense, if applied, will show you clear warning signs in a relationship. Finding out your husband or wife is leading a double life as a criminal, cheater, drug addict, or psychopath is not something you want to discover after you are married. If your eyes are not glued shut, and your head is not between your legs, you can see what and whom a person is, inside and out, over a reasonable amount of time.

Time and time again I read about bizarre love triangles between a guy who fancies himself a player, and two baby mommas. These situations never wind up with a positive result for anyone. Stop laying down with a stranger without using birth control! I do not know how much clearer we can be about this issue. It's just Responsibility 101 in my mind. Bringing a child or two into the world is a serious matter. This kind of thing should be planned correctly, putting the child's well being and future first before your own. There's an interesting concept: responsibility without complete selfishness. Hmm, can we try it a bit more? We cannot sit around the table at our upper-class country clubs and complain about the poor, uneducated, minority youths, and mentally challenged folks having babies. Let's help these people help themselves for a change. We simply must do a better job of educating people who do not know any better. We live in a free country, but at some point we have to make those who do not use one ounce of common sense understand that they will not be allowed to dump their problems, children, and financial burden on society. Adults must have actual consequences, or they will just make the same mistakes time and time again.

The simple fact is that we cannot get marriage between two members of the opposite sex to work, for many reasons, including lack of preparation. We tend to dive into things without a plan, especially when we are younger. I've got news for you: It's time to stop pointing to our youth and inexperience and using these things as excuses for failure. Over the past one hundred years, millions of others have been down the marriage and family road, with varying degrees of success or failure. We should learn from these mistakes, but we seem to ignore obvious signs. At heart, people are basically the same. We are extremely attracted to members of the opposite sex, and will do anything to be with that person. We trade moral values, core beliefs, and religious beliefs, ignoring mostly obvious warning signs about this person for sexual pleasure.

There is no doubt that we can tie these failures on a massive level, as reflected by a divorce rate as high as 65 percent in some areas of the country, to a very real lack of respect for the institution of marriage. We just simply do not take it seriously anymore. People get married first these days, then "see how things go" for a while. I have the solution to this dilemma. It's become painfully obvious that most Americans use three parts of their body when chasing members of the opposite sex. First, they use their groin area and hormones. Second, especially in the case of so many million females as they are generally more emotional than males, we use our hearts. The part of our human system we use the least is the brain. And it's a distant third, if we use it at all. Once again, Americans have things upside-down and backwards.

Sexual and physical attraction is a temporary thing at best. Ninety percent of the time, physical pleasure is going to last three months, perhaps six months, or maybe one year if you are extremely fortunate. If we know this, how can we go through the hassle of living together very briefly before a short-lived marriage? It's simple as far as I am concerned. People must use their head and then instincts and feelings, then trust their physical attractions to their mates. If everyone followed this formula, we would have far fewer broken homes, broken hearts, and confused children. Not to mention the benefits we would reap from not tying-up the US judicial system with divorce, custody, and property battles, etc. Many of these disasters could be avoided if we simply took the time to really know each another, plan and map our futures together, and spent a reasonable amount of time courting one another. Jumping into marriage and parenthood for a "trial run" is so very irresponsible, it is not funny at all.

We need to simplify things and think in black and white, because letting people do whatever they want, whenever they want, however they want to do it does not work. Families need to step in and do something about their children & siblings making such mistakes. We need to look at these situations practically, financially, and leave emotion out of it. Once again, and I hate to beat a dead horse here, common sense most certainly applies. If you have a child who wants to marry at the age of eighteen to twenty one, do not allow them to do so. The term "tough love" must be used here. We have gotten away from that big time over the past twenty five or thirty years in this country. For example, if your nineteen-year-old son or daughter is blinded by foolish lust, but in their "infinite wisdom" they mistake this purely physical attraction as true love, give them some space to learn, but stick to your guns when it comes to giving your blessing on something as important as marriage. As forty- and fifty-something parents, we have honed our instincts, lived and learned, and become wise over time. If you are faced with such a dilemma, as I am currently facing, do not baby the youngster, no matter how much you love them. You have to tell them you will not buy them a car, help with a home or apartment by cosigning, etc. Simply refusing to not pay for the wedding is not enough these days. They will simply do it in Las Vegas for fifty bucks, just to spite you.

Being a responsible parent is not easy, but it's not as hard as we so often make it out to be. Sit your young child or sibling down for a chat, tell them how things are in the real world. I am not a fool, so I know this will likely not work. With that being said, we still have to try the diplomatic way. When this does fail, cut them loose. If they are doomed to fail, let them fail without your help. The problem is that one of the two parents always takes the "good guy" approach by saying, "Oh, Herb, let him or her learn on their own, he or she is in love…I just want our child to be happy." If you take that approach, chances are good that you will have to take this child back into your home within a year, and possibly allow the dreaded "idiot son- or daughter-in-law" move in with them. Possibly a grandchild will come with this lovely package, too. What I am saying is pretty simple here. The odds of young folks making it on their own are slim to none, especially if their relationship is based on nothing more than puppy love and physical attraction. Therefore, we need to not allow ourselves to become more stressed by making a big financial investment in such a union. Buying them a car, house, apartment, furniture, and paying for an elaborate wedding will just add to the level of failure, and the kid will likely not learn his or her lesson, because you took all the risk.

This all seems harsh, as we love our children so deeply. You simply must convince yourself, as well as your spouse, that your loved one will be better off in the long run by your not helping them to fail. Just do not make it easy for them to drag out this failed marriage or living arrangement, when you know deep inside your heart that it will not last. While variety is indeed the spice of life, and one of my favorite things about human nature, we do not see much of it with young people. They are all basically the same horny, blinded-by-sex teenagers because it's new and feels great for a group of people at a certain age. We have not yet begun to define who we are as adults, so we make the same mistakes of the heart. Let's start using our heads first, people.

For those of us in the adult world, even the sharpest, most educated, alert, attentive-to-detail person can make one big mistake when it comes to marriage. The key is not doing it twice, folks. It never ceases to amaze me the sheer number of adults who came from a very similar family and educational background as most of us, who fail miserably at marriage and long-term relationships over and over. Are we actual gluttons for punishment? Do we have an inner drive to screw up time and time again? These questions eat away at our ability to set a good example for our young people. They see adults getting married for the fourth or fifth time and get the impression that we are not at all knowledgeable about such things. How can we give advice to our kids about staying together, making things work, and planning a life with their spouses when we cannot do it ourselves? It is reasonable to assume we will all make mistakes in our lifetime. The thing that is killing America at its core is that we do not seem to care how our myriad of mistakes are having an effect on others. If you coast through life with blinders on, never learning from your mistakes, it will definitely have a negative effect on the ones you love. Society looks down on failures, but that is not the reason you should strive to succeed as a wife or husband, father or mother, provider, and productive member of your community. You should do it because you want to, because you put others before yourself, and you enjoy doing so. This kind of example alone will make your offspring better young people, their children better and more productive, and so on. Remember, they look up to us, so let's get it right the first time.

Chapter 3
Smoke and Mirrors, Creative Accounting

You can fool even smart people some of the time, especially when you are very good about concealing your underhandedness. I have known for some time that the media does almost nothing to help in America's freefall into the doldrums of mediocrity. In the age of twenty-four-hour news channels, we can listen to the spew and regurgitate this garbage over and over again, all day and night—if we so choose. The only good thing we have seen recently has been the huge spotlight the media has cast on the latest corporate accounting scandals. For many years, the gurus on Wall Street and sitting in board rooms for large corporations would use the media as a tool for their own gain. The morons at CNN, MSNBC, and Fox News would report whatever they heard from company sources, most of it geared toward inflating specific company stocks. When it comes to showing false profits, inflating the stock, and painting a very pretty picture, one would think the corporate powers-that-be would have perfected their craft by the year 2008. Perhaps they have, but the debt and bad-credit animal has simply gotten too humongous to hide.

Personally, I was not surprised at all by the huge accounting scandals that crushed WorldCom, Enron, Adelphia, Tyco, and Lehman Brothers—just to name a few. Unfortunately, this could simply be the tip of the iceberg. Over the years we have seen hugely unrealistic asset reports, inflated and falsified profit reports, and had to try and read between the lines of Wall Street's huge pile of BS. You knew something had to give. Take Enron for example. What were they really selling? These guys played the stock inflation game to the hilt, without ever having any real cash flow or worthwhile assets of which to speak. These guys were crooks of the worst kind, gouging people for a necessity like energy. Everything Enron had was based on falsified current value reports, inflating the stock, and making their line of credit with the big banks grow. They were listed as a Fortune 500 company, and one of the largest and most respected places to work in Houston, which is one of America's largest cities. It was nothing but smoke and mirrors all the way. These clowns inflated the stock to ridiculous proportions, then cashed in, making the top dozen people on the top floor multimillionaires basically over night. Enron was a microcosm of Wall Street itself. It was an out-of-control monster with too much money, too fast. The problem was simple. It was all "funny money," and not real at all. These crooks were spending "future" money, all on paper, based on what they *might* be able to charge for energy in the future. It was also based on what technologies "may" be around the corner for them. Nothing but smoke and mirrors, my friends. They never had any concrete assets or a pile of cash you could see or touch. Kenneth Lay tried to say he did not know at all what was happening over there. He's dead from the stress of all this. One guy took his three hundred million or so and bolted for the South Pacific about a year before the collapse. Two other guys committed suicide. They knew what was going on, and they knew it for quite some time. If it looks like a duck, walks like a duck, and quacks like a duck, it's a damn duck!

What makes this entire scenario much, much worse is that the guys at the top of Enron not only lied to the outside stockholders, but tried to rally the in-house troops, begging them to keep buying company stock in the last few months, knowing full well the ship was sinking very fast. These guys are disgusting human beings to be sure. If there is hell, these are the people who top the VIP list to get in. Another couple of "winners" in the corporate world, making hundreds of millions of dollars almost overnight, were Bernie Ebbers and Scott Sullivan of WorldCom. These clowns went to the same school of inflated stock and lie through your teeth accounting as such geniuses as Enron's Andrew Fastow, Tyco's Dennis Kozlowski, and several other stand-up guys. WorldCom's stock fell through the floor in a matter of weeks, at the very same moment Scott Sullivan was sinking 20 million bucks into his South Florida, over-the-top, "hey, look at me" mansion. Bernie Ebbers and Mr. Sullivan, at the time of this writing are rotting in jail, and I hope they are bending over for the soap. Ebbers was extremely careful to never leave a paper, or electronic e-mail trail of any kind. Why would a person do that, unless he had much to hide? Answer: He knew what was happening all along.

The recent large-scale financial failures at Lehman Bros., Fanny Mae, Freddy Mac, Washington Mutual, etc. should scare us. I know it scares me. Even a Wall Street and stock purchasing novice like me understands a thing or two very clearly about all this. Firstly, you cannot keep raising credit lines hundreds or millions, or even billions beyond the point of no return. These things will never get paid off. The federal government is now waving its collective arms and legs frantically, asking the tax payers to bail out all these crooks. We have already done so for the insurance giant AIG and were rewarded with the big wigs at that company taking a chunk of their nearly 100 million and going to a spa in the dessert, relaxing to the tune of $450,000 or so. Nice job guys: Being a crook and poor business person at the same time is stressful work. You needed to get away for a weekend. Here is another simple fact that I cannot believe seemingly educated people even discuss on Capital Hill, etc. How in the hell can you just print more money, extend more lines of credit, and call these handouts "loans" over and over? Answer: You cannot. It will bankrupt us, possibly in the near future. It will not be long before the US dollar is nearly worthless if we keep this up. Even a junior high school student in his first year of civics knows it is not the government's role to bail out businesses and get involved with every little thing we do. Not in a true, free Democracy. Perhaps that is why we have become so lazy and nonproductive that a socialist was just elected in November 2008. This could get really ugly, long before it gets better. More taxes, more spending, and more throwing money we do not have into black holes is not the way to fix things. You cannot put a small, poorly made bandage on a gaping, large, blood-gushing wound. You have to sew it up correctly, and clean it until it's properly healed. Our leaders simply do not understand this concept.

Greed has been mans biggest downfall since the beginning of time. It just happens to be on a staggeringly larger money scale these days. I am not certain which frightens me more. Is it the fact that so many supposedly smart men and women with advanced business degrees are nothing more than highly paid crooks? Or, is it that they have eight-year degrees from prestigious universities yet they make such bad decisions? I find it very hard to believe that masters in Business Administration programs across the land have been teaching the folks at the top of these Fortune 500 companies to hide the facts, inflate the stock at all costs, and put the future of the company entirely in the hands of creditors. Whatever happened to real cash flow, smart investing, reasonable accounting practices, and pay-for-performance attitudes?

This is the only country in the modernized world that rewards failure on such staggeringly high level. CEOs, presidents, CFOs, and CIOs bounce from corporation to corporation every few years, signing seven- and eight-figure deals with no consequences if they should fail. How can anyone, much less a seemingly smart room of directors and major stockholders justify what has become known as the "golden parachute" for these clowns? A guy comes in for three years and drives the company's stock into the ground as it loses 20 to 50 percent of its value, spends a truckload of the company's money, then receives an 18-million-dollar reward on the way out the door! Ludicrous if you ask me. In other technologically advanced countries such as Japan, high-ranking corporate officials who fail on an even smaller scale than what I have mentioned here are fired, shamed, and given nothing. Moreover, they are basically blacklisted from obtaining future cushy gigs. Not in the good ole USA! We see these guys and gals leap from one job to another with piss-poor performance, but they get millions up front, during their employment, and on their way out the door, no matter how bad the performance. What a country.

The thing that really bothers me is that these are the guys and gals who were supposed to be the smartest. We looked up to them as the people who really ran the country, and even controlled the world's financial markets, middle-class salaries, stock market, and overall health of the business world. We often separated them from the crooked politicians in Washington, because we thought they had all the real cash and power. Recent scandals, criminal activity, and lack of actual cash at these corporate giants clearly proves that we cannot trust anyone with our money and jobs. How deep does this go? How many more crooked presidents, CEOs, and accounting firms have not yet gotten caught? Are they playing the same game, but are just better at the smoke and mirrors game than some of the others? This is all very worrisome to say the least. We are most definitely on shaky ground, and that ground is crumbling fast. I feel that I can provide a much less bitter perspective on all this, as I have only lost twenty-five thousand dollars or so in the market. I work with many others who have lost ten times that amount. To be honest, I have never trusted Wall Street, so I put only a small amount of my earnings into the stock market since the early 90s. Greed is perhaps the deadliest of all sins. Still, it's not an excuse for the behavior we have seen in recent years.

Being a level-headed guy, I tend to cut out all the red tape and BS. I look at things objectively, trying to not over-complicate them. Two events in modern history come to mind: one before my time, the other occurring within the last 15 years. Firstly, it's easy for me to read between the lines, remove all the different angles and opinions and apply common sense to the John F. Kennedy assassination in Dallas. I do not know anything about shooters on the grassy knoll, and whether or not they were killed within hours of the event. I have not paid really close attention to the documentaries on cable TV aired during the past twenty years that argue both sides. I have not read more than a few pages of the Warren Commission report. Who is connected to the conspiracy? Was it the mob or the Cubans? Who knows for sure, other than people who have long since passed-away. What I do know is this. If the numbers and times and reports on the weapons used are at all accurate, a world-class marksman could not have squeezed off three head shots in six seconds from the book depository, even with a non–bolt-action rifle. Lee Harvey Oswald would not have ranked in the top one hundred thousand marksmen on the planet, so he could not have pulled this off with a scope and a .50 cal. With that particular bolt-action Italian rifle, very few men could have come close to making those three shots, and Oswald was not on that list. Fact: He had help or was set up as a patsy. The evidence is plain and simple, clear and concise in my book. Jack Ruby shot Oswald in Dallas shortly afterwards.

This not a guy who hung out with pillars of the community and the local ministers. He was indeed connected to criminals, possibly the mob. Therefore, Oswald could not have been the lone shooter from the position from which "they" say he fired, and certainly he could not have carried this act out in six seconds. Moreover, the guy was not smart enough to think all this up by himself. That fact is evidence enough for me.

The other highly publicized, over-covered event of which I speak was the O.J. Simpson trial in Southern California. This guy is a piece of trash. What in his character, past, personality, or mindset could possibly make anyone think he did not commit this crime? Nicole Brown Simpson and Ronald Goldman were murdered in cold blood, and done so with obvious rage and intent. This was not a random event, and the killer is still on the loose. The clowns in the LA District Attorney's office had the right guy and let him go. Judge Lance Ito allowed the trial to become not only a media circus, but a freak show all together. He allowed the high-priced team of O.J. lawyers way too much time and freedom in hand-picking, training, coaxing, and perhaps paying off, jurors. Make no mistake, O.J. Simpson would have been found guilty on all charges within a month or three in any other state. The fact that he was tried in California was his only saving grace. They got him several years later in Nevada on kidnapping & burglary, justice served. This was all done in Southern California on the taxpayer dollar. Here's a clue, the state and county are broken to begin with, so the spineless Judge Ito should not have let this thing go on like it did. This was a shameful spectacle in US law history. It was a clear indicator of just how far the system has fallen and how corrupt and distracted from its purpose Lady Justice has become. Forget all the media-driven crap about O.J. Simpson being railroaded and framed by then LA detective Mark Furman. Forget the conspiracy theories aimed at rendering the LA County Coroner's office completely incompetent. I can even look the other way, and almost justify Mr. Simpson's pitiful alibi that he was on the midnight flight to Chicago the night of the murder for business reasons, and cut his hand on a glass in the Chicago hotel, etc. Forget the fact that O.J. was being driven by his old football buddy A.C. Cowlings to the Mexican border with a gun to his head. Certainly, a man with two children would be so distraught that his ex-wife was fooling around that he would want to join her in heaven or hell, would he not? This was obviously a bundle of lies, but I can only focus on one thing in this case. I am not a lawyer, not a criminalist, never trained as a crime scene investigator in my life. However, I can read between the lines, use my eyes, and apply common sense to things like this. The infamous white Ford Bronco was registered to only a man named Orenthal James Simpson. Contained within that Bronco were not the blood types, but the *actual blood and DNA* of Mr. Simpson and the two deceased individuals, Nicole Brown and Ron Goldman. Nobody else had blood or DNA in that vehicle, which was registered to Mr. Simpson, in case I forgot to mention that before. Only those three persons deposited blood somehow in the vehicle. Was this magic? Was it a conspiracy? Yeah, the LAPD came up with this plot and singled O.J. out for such a genius and evil plan because they hate the Buffalo Bills. Who could have done this? Answer: O.J. Simpson, that's who. I'll get beyond all that other garbage and focus on the Ford Bronco. There is no scenario in which you can explain this one away. The only other possibility would be someone with the same blood running thru his veins: OJ's oldest son.

We are spoon-fed all these crazy theories and twists by the media to keep us interested. You must use your common sense for a minute and forget the extra "fluff" and window dressing. There are three hundred or more channels on cable and satellite TV these days, with thousands of news programs, documentaries, and movies based on real life events. Moreover, this monster of an industry counts on the fact that the masses will believe anything they see or hear. They have to make things interesting for job security reasons. If people turn the TV off, actually get out and exercise one of these days, these folks will be out of a job. They are not really contributing anything positive to society as it is, so I would not lose any sleep if this should happen. This is coming from a guy who has a degree in Radio and TV Broadcasting. I worked in radio in Michigan back in the early 1990s, and I still have close friends in that field. Still, they are part of the problem, and a big part at that.

Chapter 4
Apple Pie Is All We Have Left

Baseball, apple pie, and Chevrolet...Since Major League Baseball and Chevy are dying a slow death these days, apple pie is all we have left. This is a touchy subject for me. My hero was once Chris Berman, and I had dreamed of becoming an ESPN or sports radio anchor one day. I actually touched the dream in the early 90s, working as sports director at an AM radio station near Detroit for a couple of years. Growing up in the United States, and playing baseball from little league through high school and perhaps into college, was an American dream. Baseball was as American as anything I can think of. The late owner of the Oakland A's (Charlie O. Finley) was seen as somewhat of a kook when he said, "Free Agency will ruin the game of baseball" back in the mid 1970s. He also indicated that it would only take fifteen or twenty years to do it. Man, he was right on the money. It seems that creative accounting, ridiculous salaries, golden parachutes, and outrageous debt are not exclusive to Wall Street and the mortgage industry. Major League Baseball has been losing money hand-over-fist for many years now. The general managers and owners in the big leagues just don't get it. Again, this is another glaring example of compete blindness and stupidity at the top of a once powerful and profitable industry.

I was watching an Atlanta Braves broadcast on TBS a few years back on a Wednesday evening in September. The announcers had commented a couple of times on the small crowd, expressing surprise and disappointment about the large number of empty seats at a game between two contenders so late in the season. They had also commented, not that they had to do so, on how the stadium in Atlanta had only been 60 percent full on many nights that season. They were questioned why this was so. Hello McFly, anybody home in there? The MLB season is 162 games in length. That means each team plays eighty-one regular season games in its home park. Let's see…at an average of $20 or more per seat, plus $35 for parking, $7.50 for a beer, $4.75 for a hot dog, and $5.00 for a Pepsi, you're looking at no less than $150 for a family of 4 to attend a game. And this is a game they play three and four nights in a row. You can expect to get $100 to $150 out of folks for eight games per season in an NFL city, but how can you expect to do so consistently with baseball? Answer: Do the math; it does not work, you geniuses. Minorleague ball costs about $40 for 4 tickets, 4 dogs, and 4 sodas. Do the math, morons. One does not have to be an MBA to see this is not good business.

What drives these ridiculous prices? Well, overpaid players, plain and simple. MLB owners have been signing contracts as if they were in denominations of Monopoly money or pesos for the past twenty years or so. The George Steinbrenners of the league do not see a problem with paying well-past-their-prime pitchers and position players not a mere seven figures, but eight figures in many cases. Alex Rodriguez is an every-day player, a star, and a productive player in the regular season. However, he has not produced in the post season much at all, and is only average on defense, running bases, etc. The man hits with power, drives in runs, and is somewhat popular, but is he worth twenty-five millions dollars per year? Answer: He's not realistically worth one tenth that amount. All he does is hit a baseball three times out of ten. This is not a realistic salary. The Steinbrenners and front-office guys in Boston have brought in pitchers like Roger Clemens, David Wells, Curt Schilling, and co. at bargain-basement salaries of between eighteen and twenty six million dollars. Clemens, one of the most brain-dead fools to whom I have ever listened at a press conference, was paid about fifty-two million dollars over his final two seasons with the New York Yankees. The guy was well into his forties—beyond his prime to be sure. He shows up six or eight weeks into the season with a laundry list of special requests, toting a big head and obnoxious attitude. He certainly did nothing to gain the respect of his teammates with such antics. Such a huge salary is justified in what manner? He won an average of twelve games those last two years, his ERA was higher, his strikeout totals lower, and he did nothing worth mentioning in the post season. For twenty-six million bucks, the man should have cured cancer, solved the world hunger crisis, and cleaned up the pork in DC. Instead, he wallowed in mediocrity, hanging around past his usefulness because somebody with a ton of money was dumb enough to pay him.

Baseball was really hurting in the 90s but did nothing to squelch the spiraling-out-of-control salary problem. Free agents just kept getting more and more each off season, despite the fact that baseball was losing five hundred million or more each year. Pro sports is one of the most poorly run, scratch-your-noggin-and-say-"huh" industries on the planet. Major League Baseball is at the top of the list. Where else can you use this kind of logic? Teams continue to lose money by the truckload, as the stands are empty. Most of the league has no real television money of which to speak, save for the Yankees, Red Sox, Angels, Dodgers, and Cubs. Despite all that, owners weasel the tax payers into footing the entire bill, or paying for half of a new six-hundred-million dollar park that nobody will come to either. Let me see…If I had a small hot-dog cart at the corner of Fifty-fifth and Seventh that had been losing money for ten straight years, what should I do? If I went to the bank with plans to build a new cart, ten times the size of the current disaster and just across the street, they would laugh till they cried, then have security toss me in the street.

Not in the world of MLB and big time sports. The Arizona Diamondbacks of the National League enjoyed a certain level of success in their first few years of existence in the league, winning a World-Series title over the Yankees a few years back. However, much like the Florida Marlins, also a successful club, the

Diamondbacks were not drawing many fans, and losing millions and millions of dollars. The solution? They came up with a plan to have the tax payers spend $414 million on new digs. The problem? The taxpayers in Maricopa County turned the measure down by a resounding percentage. The Diamondbacks would not be denied, as they needed someone other than their wealthy owner to foot the bill for the two salaries he decided to pay old-guy starting pitchers Randy Johnson and Curt Schilling. He needed to payover twenty million to each. Even though a good majority of the taxpayers in Maricopa Country cannot afford to attend a game, and certainly could not afford to shell out the extra seventy dollars per person that year in state taxes, the good ole boys (Arizona Governor and Diamondbacks owner, Ken Kendrick) got together, greased a few palms, and found a legal loophole. *Heck, them silly taxpayers don't know what they want! They did not mean it when they shot down the bill for a new stadium almost four to one. They really want to pay for it, so let's make them do it!* And they laughed all the way to the bank. Nowadays, you can hang out in the pool beyond right field for a mere two thousand dollars or so. If you're not that fancy, come out and pay thirty-five dollars for parking, and sixty six dollars for a pair of half-decent seats, pardner! They won't be hard to get.

Then there was MLB's saving grace, led by one of the most obvious puppets for the top three or four owners in pro sports history, Mr. Bud Selig. They raised the mound, enlarged the strike zone, juiced up the ball, corked some bats, and started them a home-run-derby frenzy. At the forefront, steroid kings Mark McGwire and "Cork-Swingin'" Sammy Sosa. Even guys like Louis Gonzales (one hundred and seventy pounds soaking wet) got into the act, belting fifty homers. It is pretty funny how he never hit more than nineteen or twenty previously in his baseball life. McGwire and Sosa did not stop there; no sir. They hit fifty-five, sixty, then seventy homers! Yippee! There is only one problem: They cheated— almost all of them. Hank Aaron and Babe Ruth hit 1,500 homers collectively and all they were juiced-up on was cigars, beer, and Corn Flakes. Guys like Palmiero, McGwire, Sosa, and Bonds—now the new home-run record holder—all cheated. As if putting the already watered-down crop of MLB pitchers at clear disadvantages was not enough, these guys were all doing steroids. They were enhancing their power with pills and needles—very nice. Like I had described in the previous chapter, the baseball gurus were cheating. Everyone knew it, that they were driven by greed. *Gotta make that money, so we will turn the other cheek,* they figured. Heck, like Mark McGwire said, "Yes, I took that, but it was not on the banned substance list at the time." No problem then, because like most Americans who get caught with their hand in the cookie jar, those guys simply had to say, "Everyone else was doing it; why not me?" time and time again. The press just ate it up. Once again, an excellent example our role models and sports heroes for our children. I am going somewhere with this.

Man is by nature a very weak species. This is why we make so many mistakes, and we do so more than once. If you dangle one hundred million dollars in front of an athlete in his mid to late thirties, he's going to do whatever it takes to get that obscene amount of cash. He will never have to work another day in his life after signing said contract. The owners have created a monster with no morals, no limits, no lack of greed, and no conscience. Gimme, gimme, gimme, more, more, more. Manny Ramirez actually believes he is worth thirty million dollars per year. Think about that for a moment. He wants to be paid more money than just about any ten of us will make in our combined lifetimes, for six months of playing a kids game. The salaries have created such swollen heads on these guys they can barely fit through airport screening machines. Most professional athletes have an IQ of less than 125. If you dangle this kind of coin in front of them, all thoughts of pressure, what is right, and the state of a once-great pastime no longer matter one bit.

As I pointed out in the JFK and OJ examples in the previous chapter, let's examine Mr. Barry Bonds. Here is a guy who has never been considered a team player, and has been called selfish, self-centered, perhaps even cocky by his teammates many times in the past. How can we even question whether or not he committed perjury when he started that he never took steroids? I spent six days a week for ten years in the gym. There were only 2,800 to 3,000 guys in America stronger than I was about six years ago. Barry Bonds was not one of those guys. It's not humanly possible to put on fifty pounds in your chest in one summer without using some sort of enhancer. If it looks like a duck, walks like a duck, quacks like a duck, and smells like a duck, it's a damn duck! Several players, acquaintances, and even friends testified that they actually saw Bonds use steroids, and sold them to him. I do not even need such evidence to be convinced on this matter. No man in the history of baseball started hitting "mammoth-shot homers" after his thirty-eighth birthday. Just remove yourself from the rest of the BS and look at how many home runs Bonds clubbed at a distance of over 425 feet in his career. Then look at the percentage of those bombs hit after he ballooned up after his thirty ninth and fortieth birthdays, etc. The proof is right there that he cheated. As far as I am concerned, a huge asterisk should go into the record books next to Barry Bonds' name. This is far too sacred a record to be tainted this way. Honestly, I would feel the same way, even if Bonds were not an arsehole off the field.

Then there is the brilliant Mr. Clemens. Yes, Professor Clemens took lying and cheating to a new level. One more shining example of the kind of heroes our youth have to embrace these days. Mr. Clemens should be forever the measuring stick for the show "America's Dumbest Criminals." The world was ready to pounce all over Barry Bonds as its centerpiece for the "steroid and cheating" era in professional baseball. Man, is this guy a moron! After hearing of the latest cheating and steroid accusations, not related to his having cheated on his wife multiple times, Professor Clemens stuck his hands way up in the air and said, "Hey, pick me. Forget about Bonds and McGwire—pin this whole steroids thing on me!" Good idea, you moron. The most mind-boggling part of all this was Mr. Clemens refusal to take very simple legal advice, and simply say, "Yes, I took steroids while recovering from an injury a few years back," like his friend Andy Petitte did. Instead, Doctor Clemens looked a man thirty times smarter than himself in the eye during the hearings and proclaimed, "I did not take what all these other people say I took, sir." Despite a mountain of solid evidence and testimony. and a somewhat sympathetic panel that gave Mr. Clemens plenty of opportunities to not lie, the genius looked these guys and the camera in the eye and said, "They mis-remembered." "I cannot say they lied, because they are good folks and certainly smarter and more honest than I could ever be," President Clemens would go on to say. *They simply mis-remembered the facts y'all.* Yep, that is what happened, sir. If you believe that one, you also believe O.J. Simpson was framed for all the crimes with which he was charged.

Does a corked bat really make a difference? The so-called experts are split on this matter, saying it may or may not provide a noticeable boost in power for hitters. Sammy Sosa apologized for using a corked bat once. The opposing team and umpire noticed the cork in his bat, and I believe he was fined or suspended for a whole game. Of course, Sammy told the media and all his fans that he only had a few "batting practice" bats, and claimed that this one time only the batting practice bat somehow wound up in his hands during a real game. I will certainly not say that Sammy Sosa is a mental midget of legendary stature like Mr. Clemens. Heck, most consider Sammy to be a pretty nice fellow. Still, nobody will ever really know how many home runs he clubbed with a corked bat. His name will forever be tied to the "steroid and cheaters" era in MLB. That is pretty much the main thing anyone will remember about the guy.

Baseball Commissioner Bud Selig and the rest of the nitwits can pretend all they want that all is well with the game, but those of us with two good eyes and half a brain can see that it is not. When we were kids, everyone talked about the playoffs and the World Series. Most kids would stay up till midnight on a school night to watch the World Series, even if their team was not in it. This past October, nobody watched outside of the Philadelphia and Tampa Bay areas. Around the water cooler at work, I may see twenty people through the course of the day having a quick chat. Maybe three of those folks mentioned the World Series. A once-sacred American pastime reduced to a steroid-driven, well overpaid, brush–it–under–the rug–afterthought. The geniuses at the top of the game, amazingly led by half-wit Bud Selig, have no real national TV contract, and are extremely fortunate if 3 percent of Americans watch them on their biggest stage—the World Series.

The NBA is not far behind, with more than its share of eight-figure guys with average skills and stats. The league also has trouble drawing much of a television audience these days. Still, the brain surgeons and rocket scientists in the league's front office, along with the NBA team owners, continue to do things the American way each and every year. *Just throw more money at it, things will get better.* Man, we certainly take the old adage "You have to spend money to make money" to extreme limits these days. Left-handed starting pitcher C.C. Sabathia signed with the Yankees for $161 million over just seven years. Despite very tough financial times right next door on Wall Street, the highest jobless rate in years, and a recession country-wide, the Steinbrenner clan chose to make this guy the highest paid pitcher ever. He throws a friggin' ball thirty-five games per year! In the wealthy man's fantasy land, this must not be a ton of money, and he's just going to figure out how to pay for it later. After all, that is the American way.

Chapter 5
Pretending to Be Big Shots

Wearing an Italian suit, carrying a five-hundred-dollar leather briefcase, wearing expensive shoes, and eating seventy-five-dollar lunches on the corporate card obviously means that person knows what he or she is doing, correct? Well, these folks tend to look the part, but have apparently been fooling us for many years. As I stated earlier, it is very likely the latest Wall Street scandals and corporate meltdowns could very well be just the tip of the iceberg. The media reports on these matters over and over again, until we tire of such bad news. Corporate bean counters have been getting caught with their hands in the virtual cookie jar for many, many years, so this is nothing new. What irks me more than anything is the rising cost of all this. The cost of attending an MBA at a smaller school is quite high, never mind the cost at an Ivy or wellrespected private institution. We must face the facts where this huge mess is concerned, as it is crippling the world economy as we speak. The American way of doing business, at its very core, has likely been broken for many years. Could we have spent billions on training and higher education to teach these leaders how to cheat, lie, steal, and pass the buck? It would appear so. Just how deep does it go? I am very much afraid we do not really want to know the answer to that particular question.

Big business is what they call it. As we are so painfully discovering, we may be forced to refer to the current era as the "big scam" or "bailout decade" or something much worse. The message we will be sending to current and future businesses if this current seven-hundred-billion-dollar bailout of the mortgage and auto industries is indeed allowed to take place, it is a very dangerous one. People, this is a very bad idea. We have already proven that our corporate business people cannot be trusted. We have seen firsthand how extending massive credit lines, then re-extending even more, then restructuring in bankruptcy courts, etc. does not work. The message a massive bailout sends is simple: "Do not worry about cutting costs, trimming spending, reducing bonus programs, or changing your overall business policies, guys, 'cause the taxpayers will bail you out when you fail." The people in charge of several large corporations in big trouble these days simply do not get it. We already touched upon the morons at AIG, and what they did with the taxpayers' generosity. Just a matter of weeks later, we see the three CEOs from Ford, Chrysler, and General Motors take private and corporate jets from Detroit to Washington to ask the taxpayers for another several hundred billion to bail out the failing auto industry. This may be an even larger scam than the Wall Street mess. I am betting these clowns did not have black coffee and a small bag of peanuts in flight like the rest of us. Spending twenty thousand dollars to fly in ultimate luxury to DC so you can ask the taxpayers and lawmakers for a huge handout is not something I can put into words. It is disgusting beyond comprehension. I have to fly coach much of the time. So these guys cannot fly commercial, maybe even first class, for seven hundred dollars or so? Lord knows that ninety-minute flight is rough and they needed the comfort of a leather recliner, fully stocked bar, and filet mignon for such a long journey. Simply put, the American automakers have managed things poorly. Take GM for example. Not too long ago, they were the world's largest, richest, most successful, and supposedly most profitable auto maker. Why have GM and Ford failed so miserably? There are more cars on the road today than ever before. Look on your own street in any suburban American town, and you will see GM and Ford cars and trucks aplenty. It seems that there is a Ford Explorer or pickup truck in one out of every three or four driveways in any given middle-class neighborhood. Look at the house next door, and you will likely see a Chevy Blazer, Suburban, or Cadillac Escalade. Out on the roads, you see another one hundred million lower-priced, mid-sized, and compact GM and Ford products all over the place. And they are losing money? How is this possible without people at the top doing a terrible job? Answer: It's not possible. They have made and spent billions and failed to save for a rainy day. The aforementioned CEO's have basked in luxury while at the very moment they have "cut costs" by laying off many thousands of workers.

Here's a hint for you wizards. Make a product that you cannot lose money on. Does it make sense to sell a Pontiac Sunbird or Grand Am for a mere $13,500 if the piece of crap does not have a chance in hell of making it beyond the warranty period? No, it certainly does not. Because you have to repair the car at your own costs, perhaps two or three times or more. This makes no sense when your initial profit was only $1,800 or so. Toyota sells millions of Camry's and other cars all over the world. The Camry has been the top selling auto for what, twelve years running now? I travel to Germany once or twice each year. While there, I travel by private car and taxi. The Mercedes Benz in a very expensive automobile, but it outperforms anything we make in America. Ditto for BMW, Toyota, Nissan, Honda, and the list gos on and on. When Lexus or BMW sells one of their finer cars for a set price, they know they are selling quality for that price. The BMW 7-Series Limo sells for approximately $117,000 and change, last I checked. You buy this car, it comes fully-loaded, and you will not be disappointed. Moreover, BMW backs this car to the hilt, and protects their own investment by building any current and future costs for maintenance and repairs into the selling price. What a concept indeed. They know for certain they are going to make $40,000 profit, and the buyer has no problem with that.

If the brain surgeons in Detroit want to get it right, a good start would be to stop selling junk for a low price that they will have to keep repairing over and over again. This makes no business sense. Each and every day over the past fifteen to twenty years, I have made a mental note of what I see abandoned, broken down, or burned to a crisp on the side of American highways. It would be quite impossible for me to count them in a completely accurate manner, but I can tell you than a high percentage of those hunks of junk have been Pontiac models. I have seen hundreds and hundreds of broken-down Grand Ams, Firebirds, Sunbirds, and other poorly made models over the years. Conversely, I can count the number of Toyotas, Nissans, and BMWs sitting on the shoulders on one or two hands. Mass-producing junk just does not make sense to me. Business 101 would dictate that you make a top-notch, or at least decent, product, stand behind it, and make sure it lasts X number of years, would it not? One thing the corporate world has prided itself on over the years is being politically correct. What this means is that they have gotten really good at passing the buck, pointing the finger elsewhere, and accepting responsibility for nothing. We blame everyone but ourselves, but cannot point the finger of blame in any specific direction. "Our official statement is as follows: Acme Corporation can neither confirm nor deny anything at this time." It certainly is nice to have a built-in excuse for everything. The official statement from each of the (once) big three automakers, now known as the little begging three, were similar in nature as they responded to being grilled on Capitol Hill by lawmakers on November 19, 2008. Each corporate information officer, or, better known as BS-spewing-flunky for the CEOs, claimed that each of their big shots flew corporate jets to DC at twenty thousand dollars or so per trip because it is a "safety matter," and that company policy would likely not change on business-related travel for the higher ups. I guess by "matter of safety" they mean that their big shots are public figures and cannot travel amongst the common man, lest he may be persecuted by the common, simple folk. I certainly hope so, jerks. They actually think we are all dumb enough to not know what they really mean is this: "Hey, we can do whatever we want to do, as you need us more than we need you. If you do not bail us out, we will close up shop, so no more crappy cars." Good riddance, but we likely will not be that lucky.

This is a tough subject for me to be so negative about, as I grew up in Southeastern Michigan. I was born in Detroit, and most of my friends and family members still live in that area. Watching the good people in that area struggle so mightily with unemployment, foreclosures, and an overall poor economic out-look hurts. Still, I do not think bailing out the auto makers, and letting them go back to business as usual is a fix at all. That would temporarily jump start things, but the reality is that the Motown area needs to not be so dependent upon a very broken Big Three at its core. It will take many years to fix this—if it can be fixed at all. We should be shocked and completely disgusted that the big three top dogs chose to fly on three separate corporate jets to DC so they could beg for twenty-five billion dollars or more in bailout funds. The truly sad thing is that I am not at all surprised by this kind of thing any longer. Let's see, how many years of college education are between the guys sitting at the top of the GM Ren Cen, the Ford Headquarters in Dearborn, and the Daimler-Chrysler building in Troy, Michigan? Now, add the combined years of their VP's assistants, and other corporate flunkies, and you get maybe two thousand years of college and experience. Yet, not one of them said to the other, "Hey guys and gals, let's all take one jet to DC, as it might look bad otherwise." Not a shred of common sense between the entire bunch of highly paid nitwits. The auto industry is just one shining example of America trying to put a small band aid on a large, open wound. The wound requires major surgery, reconstruction, and perhaps a complete overhaul, so a bandage is certainly not going to work. The same goes for our healthcare system, the airline industry, Wall Street, insurance companies, and the list goes on for quite a stretch of land. I certainly do not have all the answers. This will take many, many years, and it will likely not be completely fixed in my lifetime. However, I can tell you where to start. First of all, what the hell does a board of directors actually do? They most certainly do not protect the interests of the average stockholder. From what I have seen with the automakers, they direct which moron will lead their company into the ground, and pay him very well. Forget the politics. Forget bean counting and political schmoozing, who knows whom, etc. Those things should be way down the list of requirements for a strong leader. Numbers one and two on that list for a successor for these clowns running things now should be integrity and common sense. Let's be smart and hire a man or woman with perhaps a bit less experience kissing babies and kissing butt, and instead thoroughly checking their background to see what kind of person they are. Will they do whatever it takes to get the company back on its feet, and accept only pay-for-performance terms, nothing more, nothing less? Yes, I mean take a small, reasonable salary, perhaps five hundred thousand dollars with bonuses and stock options, but if things improve. I think most of us could feed our families, drive two or three decent cars, and pay the mortgage on that kind of salary. What we have done over the past fifty years or more is basically flush hundreds of billions of dollars down the toilet in guaranteed salary money. If you start making people perform and get positive results for their pay, they will take a personal interest in seeing that things work they way they should, or leave at the end of the year, without a golden parachute.

How can we sit in front of our big screen TVs, read the daily paper, or surf the web on a daily basis and not see that all this is tied together. For many years now, we have been rewarding failure. That's right, paying folks with huge salaries, bonuses, stock options, and perks when they don't even create positive results. The old attitude that this kind of thing is far too complex for us common folk to understand is not working. You people are supposed to be smart, sitting up there on the top floor of your high rise. But, as you have shown over and over again, you're not that smart at all. We do understand too well. It's time for you to do things in a completely different manner. We sit around on twenty-four-hour news networks and talk shows with all these useless opinions, listing "Expert" next to the names of the guests, etc. And if they are actually an expert on the matter and can fix something, anything at all, they should be hired to do so. That is my fix for many of these issues. We do not need political people running our most important industries, corporations, and companies. We need people with strong, real, actual business experience. Somewhere along the way, we started hiring politicians to run things, and this particular skill set does not translate well into each and every type of business. Just because a man or woman knows how to dress like a big shot, speak with confidence, and smile while they lie through their teeth, does not mean he or she can productively run the company.

It is time to hold some of the "good ole boys" accountable for their actions. These boys have sat in their country clubs, limos, spas, and private jets for many a year, literally laughing at how stupid middle class Americans actually are. They not only laugh, but depend on the fact that we will always throw our large amount of expendable income at things we do not actually need. These guys sit poolside, sipping thirty-seven-dollars-a-glass red wine as they laugh at the way we will spend money on anything. They count on us to purchase things of which we already have five or six, not knowing any better. When the heads of the big three car makers go to Capital Hill on private, luxury jets and step out with a tin cup in their hands, it does not paint a pretty image of corporate America. Worse yet, they did not have a solid figure of cash in mind to keep their companies from folding. These guys went to college for how many years? They were also asked by the senate committee if this ballpark figure of money would guarantee they would make it to March 31, 2009. The geniuses did not have a real answer for that one either. With these guys at the helm, is it any wonder Detroit is in real trouble? Only the strong survive, so we need to get much, much stronger at the top, and do so quickly.

These boys and girls have to stop going through the motions, quit pretending to be important, and actually come up with some solutions. If the guy wearing forty-dollar cotton pants and a Wal-Mart collared shirt has a better idea than the guy in the room with a fifteen-hundred-dollar Italian suit on, then let's listen to him. If the woman with very little in the area of political expertise walks into the boardroom, fresh out of community college, wearing shoes from Sears has a better idea than the Ivy League gal who shops at Bloomingdales, then give her a real shot. Some of this stuff is not "rocket science" or "brain surgery," people: Just do the right thing. Take fewer risks and stop worrying about image and politics before the company bottom line. Instead of conducting business as usual, waiting for bailouts, changing names, moving departments around, and being a completely reactive business, let's be proactive, plan for any and all scenarios, come up with profitable ideas, and get the right people in the offices on the top floor.

Bottom line: US auto makers pay much higher salaries and benefits than foreign car makers on average. Our auto industry CEOs and VPs are paid millions more than their counterparts overseas. Get over it, you guys: You are going to have to make a better product, take less money for a while, get paid for performance, and understand that the union only protects the salaries and jobs of so many. At a certain point if things continue the way they are, the company will eliminate all jobs, and go belly-up. What good will the union do then? Sacrifices will have to be made, plain and simple. In the past, the big shots in Detroit did not listen to the workers or the consumers. That is not smart business, no matter which way you slice it.

The recently proposed twenty-five-billion-dollar bailout makes no sense at all. Simply put, almost everyone in America drives a car. If the powers that be at Ford, GM, and Chrysler knew what they were doing and put out a good product, there is no way they could lose money. They have mishandled their own money for years, so why would they take better care of the taxpayers' free cash? Answer: They won't.

Chapter 6
Television: A True Idiot Box

Wow, is there some garbage on TV these days! That is an under-statement in every sense of the word. America is literally getting lazier and dumber by the day as we soak-up the senseless drivel on our airways. From American Idol to Survivor to The Pickup Artist, we have sunk to an all-time low. This stuff is so bad, I can hear the brain cells being killed by the millions as our teens and some adults watch a single hour of network television. It's not just that the ideas and concepts themselves are really bad, but the subjects, or "reality TV stars" as to whom they are referred—Man, could they find people with less flare and personality? Is that even possible? I have found myself sitting in a room all alone, nobody home by me, so I click on one of the aforementioned shows for five minutes or so. Some of the guests on the show are so embarrassingly pathetic and ignorant, I find myself covering my eyes because I am so embarrassed for them. This is how far Hollywood has sunk. The current slate of reality TV crap is so repetitive, so dull, so void of creativity, we might as well be watching home movies of our least favorite aunts and uncles in the sixties. This programming is so bad I would truthfully rather sit through a six-hour insurance seminar.

With very few exceptions, there has been very little worth watching on network television for the past several years. While there are several worthwhile, educational, interesting programs on cable and satellite channels like: Discovery, Travel, History, and a few others, many others have forgotten the very basic concept that TV is supposed to be entertaining. The only thing worse than reality TV may be entertainment TV type programs. How can you stretch this crap into thirty or sixty minutes? It's absolutely mindboggling that people even with a high school education will sit in front of the idiot box and watch with great interest a thirty-minute discussion on whether or not Britney Spears is a good mom or not. They follow that up with an hour long discussion about whether or not Brad Pitt and George Clooney shop at the same place. Wake the fu** up people! This kind of thing is so unimportant, it's hardly worth ten seconds worth of even the most bored person's time at the water cooler on Monday morning. Really, no, anyone with a job, family, and one or two hobbies should not even think about such things. If you have any kind of life of your own, watching such programs would not even be on your radar. Get up and go do anything else, people! Doing yard work, or mopping the floor a second time is more fun that a hearing a discussion on Madonna's underwear collection. Get a life!

Then we have good ole MTV. Remember when they actually played videos? The programming in recent years must be interesting to the fourteen to nineteen, unemployed, and high-school dropout demographic, because I can see no value in this at all. MTV and VH1 have been on a roll, downhill. Watching something like *Tyron's Hip Hop Beach, I Gots Me More Stuff in My Crib Than U Be Havin'*, or *Who Is Actually Diseased and Desperate Enough to Sleep with Flava-Flav this week?* is almost like getting beat with a wet hose for eight hours. In fact, I'll take the hose. VH1 Classic is still pretty good, but it seems the morons running it have decided to lean toward the MTV style programming a bit. They dug up a very washed-up ex-lead singer of Poison(Brett Michaels), carted in thirty or fourty bimbos from the nearest LA STD clinic, and figured people would buy the "true love" format. Let me tell you, I do not want to meet anyone who watched this one more than twice. I try to keep an open mind and be objective, so that I can form an actual opinion on this kind of thing. So, I sat through an hour, maybe seventy minutes worth of the program. Without exaggerating much, I would say the smartest whore on this show had an IQ of ninety-two or ninety-three. These gals had real talent, such as: putting their leg behind their head, painting nails, showing the target tattoos on their lower backs to strangers, applying medicated vaginal itch cream, and laughing like drunken baboons. A few of these bimbos had STDs the medical community has not even come up with names for as of yet. Brett, I hope you wore at least three condoms, and had penicillin on hand.

Jerry Springer certainly has company these days. How long has Maury Povich been on the air? How many times can he bring mentally challenged street trash to try and figure out which one of the eighty guys she had un-protected sex with is her baby's daddy? How long can this trash go on? Also, it seems any halfwit with a law degree from Cancun Community College can get his or her own "Judge Reality" show. Yeah, this is great entertainment. Two retards suing and countersuing each another for $350 cell-phone bills. The thing that is not so funny is that Americans are actually this dumb. We do indeed tie up the courts with such time-wasting garbage. The problem is too many channels. When all the good ideas have been done a dozen times over, and there are twenty-four hours in a day and three hundred channels to fill, this is the result. We get programming that is literally making us less intelligent. We get no-personality, no-intellect trash on TV day after day.

Hollywood would lead you to believe that all is well. People still have expendable income and free time, even in a down economy. So, let us keep putting out movies, even without any fresh ideas. Everything has been written that can be written. There are only so many words in the English language, so many plots, so many genres, etc. Our motion picture industry has quite frankly run out of ideas. How many different ways can seventy-year-old actors blow up the same thing? I guess another few thousand, from the looks of things. We do see some decent nonfiction movies, but those true stories with just the right cast have become few and far between these days. I do not know about you, but I am pretty tired of 1970s sitcoms being turned into a two-hour movie. The sad reality is that Hollywood has run out of creative ideas. The reason most of today's films seem all-too-familiar is simple: They are familiar. Many of the plots are not only similar, but often the same. More often than not, it is pretty easy to figure out how a movie is going to end, because you feel as though you saw it coming in some other flick.

Much of my ranting in this chapter may seem just like my bitter opinion, but I do have an actual point to make. The information age has mesmerized America to the point where we spend a large chunk of our lives sitting in front of one type of video screen or another. People who work on desktop and laptop PCs forty or fifty hours a week tend to not be on their home PCs as much, but spend another fifty hours or more watching TV at home, on the road, and even on vacation. Those who do not work at a desk tend to spend a great deal of their time at home on the internet, watching TV, and renting DVDs. Not only is it seemingly easy for any halfwit to land a gig on a Judge or reality TV show, it seems just as easy to get a talk show. With three hundred or more channels out there being watched 'round the clock, the talent bar has definitely been lowered. We Americans are definitely creatures of habit, so we get stuck in a rut quite easily. Here is some good advice for many of my fellow lazy Americans: Oprah does not know squat! Such personalities may be rich, but sitting on the couch and taking advice on real life matters within your own household from Oprah Winfrey, Jerry Springer, or Tyra Banks is not helping anyone. We must remember that people love to hear themselves talk, and love to see themselves on TV even more. Television personalities have learned to act out their emotions with what seems like very real passion, interest, and flare. None of this applies to your household or life situation, people, so turn the TV off. The aforementioned TV folks, along with Dr. Phil and others, are just trying to sell themselves, and put a few more million in the bank. The more you watch, the more they make. The more you watch them, the better chance they have of selling the heck out of another self-promoting book at $29.95 per copy. They are not helping you. They are not helping anyone but themselves. Take responsibility for your own actions. Approach your issues with common sense and make a plan of action that works for you. Besides, Dr. Phil is not even a licensed doctor, so what can he really fix? Not much in the real world, but he can certainly pad his bank accounts at our expense.

News-media is driven by negativity, ratings, and corporate interests. They report the negative news as quickly as possible, trying to add as much drama as they possibly can. None of this drivel will help you either. If you are a person with a negative, glass-is-half-empty-type of personality, watching the depressing twenty-four-hour news channels will likely not improve your outlook on life. So, I would suggest doing something else with your time. The vast majority of the people we see on TV and on the big screen are very self-centered, out-of-touch-with-reality, "It's-all-about-*me*"-type individuals. These people will do anything on and off the screen to keep attention and focus on them at all times. No moral integrity; plastic surgery on at least three body parts; one or more current addictions, and no marriage having lasted longer than two years in your past. These are things the Hollywood gurus look for on an actor's resume.

American Idol became on overnight sensation. The wildly popular show on Fox Network is yet another fine example of how we have lost our creative edge on the rest of the world. At least 95 percent of the contestants have zero talent, and the other 5 percent are qualified only to perform on a mediocre cruise line. That being said, they do fit right in with the judges. The drugged-out, rode-hard-and-put-away-wet Paula Abdul, along with her two friends, Randy and Simon, are about as exciting as a rerun of Meet the Press. Where did this Randy Jackson clown emerge from? This guy has less personality and flare than bill collector. These people are the current face of the amateur music industry? Now I completely understand why no decade will ever approach the 70s for musical talent. To think that one hundred million Americans or more actually planned to watch this show each week is really disconcerting. This is what we are doing instead of taking a walk or doing homework with our kids, and we wonder why the country is in crisis right now.

I am not a fool. I fully realize that there are three-hundred-million-plus people in the country, and we all need to make a living somehow. Therefore, when you consider the sheer number of scripts written, shows pitched, and movie treatments sent to producers over the past fifty years, it's easy to grasp the reality that most of the really good ideas have been done to death. When that occurs in any industry, the people making a living within said industry will have to reinvent the wheel, so to speak. However, we have become so entrenched in the Hollywood world of fantasy that we have lost our identity. It seems everyone in Southern California is trying to be something or somebody they are not. Poor self-esteem in LA is a multi-billion dollar industry. People there spend enough on plastic surgery and visits to their personal shrinks to easily solve the world's hunger problems ten times over. This is one of the things that absolutely dumbfounds me when I think about it. You see how poorly many celebs run their own private lives each and everyday on the news, in the paper, magazines, or whatever the source may be. Why do we want to be like them? Why would any educated, halfway intelligent human being want to be as bad as the stars are at the everyday things we take for granted like parenting and marriage? If we looked up to these people just for fame and money, I could understand the fascination with them.

The reality is that we have become even more intrigued with their pathetic private lives, purchasing tabloid magazines by the millions, and watching behind-the-scenes entertainment shows several hours per week than we are with our own lives. This is simply not a productive way to spend your time. You have your own life; worry about it. Being a good parent, good spouse, productive coworker, good friend, and a helpful member of your community is important. This is real life, so concentrate on it before you worry about how many illegitimate kids a certain celeb has with another.

You only have to take a look at some of the names celebs have come up with for their children in recent years, and you can easily see many of them are not playing with a full deck. Either that or they were wacked out on PCP and whiskey when they named the poor child. This kind of thing speaks of their selfish nature. When naming a child something completely foolish, they know all too well it will make headlines, get talked about for a few weeks, and draw more attention to them. The "me, me, me" syndrome takes priority over what the poor kid will endure the first eighteen years of his or her life having to walk around with that ridiculous name. Just Google the names of Brad Pitt's and Ashlee Simpson's children, and you will see what I am talking about. The whole Hollywood lifestyle— not unlike that of a professional athlete— is definitely part of America's problematic image. Like the aforementioned athletes and corporate big wigs, we tend to reward failure and controversy with monetary bliss. How many times was Robert Downey Jr. in and out of rehab for drugs and booze? Was it five, ten, or more? Since those court-ordered slaps on the wrist, his star has never shined brighter. I believe the man has raked in twenty million or so his last two movies alone. If he gets hammered and runs over a child on Hollywood Boulevard, perhaps he will land the lead role in the next huge blockbuster film. Well, he will have to endure ten days in the country club, ah, I mean rehabilitation clinic first. Nice work, if you can get it. Look at guys like Tom Cruise, Jim Carey, and Kevin Costner. They have easily nailed down one hundred million bucks between them the past few years combined. Can you name two really good movies they have starred in? Yes, I thought not. I do not know whom are youth should really look up to these days, but I do know it is not most actors, musicians, and celebrities.

Chapter 7
Racism In America: Still a Major Issue?

We have recently witnessed history in the United States of America. The people elected Senator Barack Obama from Illinois to be our next president. He happens to be of mixed race: His mother is white, and his father is black. Although Mr. Obama is referred to as an African American, he does represent what has become a much larger contingent of mixed races here in North America. Like millions of others, I have sat at a desk, smack dab in the middle of Corporate America for the past twenty years. During this time period, I have witnessed a few very real changes in overall attitude toward black people. Here in the deep Southern US, we would be crazy to think that racism is gone completely. You still hear the underlying hatred between the races in the speech and tone of some people. However, that percentage of old-school hatred and racism has dwindled quite a bit. Obama seems to be a pretty sharp guy, although I take that fact with a grain of salt with all politicians, regardless of party affiliation. I have not seen or read about a politician in my lifetime who was not like a Cheshire cat: lying and cheating, so I will wait a few years before passing judgment on the new president elect.

Like many middle-class Americans with a bit of education, an ability to form an informed opinion, and an open mind, I have a heckuva lot more issue with the fact that Obama is a socialist than I do with his race. Personally, I did not cast a vote for either the republican or democrat ticket. I voted for someone else, as is my right. Obama steps all over the constitution.

There will no doubt be a large contingen of Americans who will not look past Obama's skin color. That fact cannot be debated. However, he will be given a chance by most people to succeed for the very same reason he won the election by a somewhat-comfortable margin without having any real plan. People were simply ready for something else. In the history of American politics, the incumbent has never stood a chance when the economy takes such a downward turn, especially if that nosedive occurs mostly in the last year before the election takes place. The Democrats could have picked almost anyone and likely won. Picking Obama and using one simple word, *change,* without really saying what they were going to change how they were planning to change it, or when they would do so, was a brilliant move by Obama and his people. With the jobless rate up, the stock market down, and many financial crises ongoing, all he had to do was say the word *change* and seem sincere about it. The only problem I have with this past election, not unlike the few others of which I have been a part, was simple ignorance on the part of the young voters. I have no problem with them voting for whomever they choose, but the face of this election was really "anybody but another old white guy," plain and simple. The majority of the voters under the age of twenty-five could not answer basic questions about Obama like age, hometown, how many were in his family, etc. But, they knew they did not want McCain, who was viewed as a Bush-like Republican drone. Personally, I feel we have come a long way in the fight against racism in this country. There are many "unspoken" views that white people have about African Americans, and many more that we openly speak about. For starters, the hard-working people in the middle class just want to see folks fend for themselves, work hard, pay their taxes, and keep their homes and yards looking decent, etc. That applies to anyone, regardless of color. I am certain there remains a very real suspicious attitude toward many people of Middle Eastern and Muslim distinctions here, as the tragedies of

September 11, 2001, are still fresh in our minds. Growing up in Detroit, we interfaced with blacks, Arabs, Orientals, and Hispanics on a daily basis. Crime was a very large problem in Detroit and still is today. It may be perceived that crime follows specific races, but everything in America comes down to money. The more money people have, the nicer the neighborhood, and you can generally count upon less crime.

Quite simply put, poor people are more upset about their place in the world, want something for nothing, and sometimes are willing to take it illegally. In my view, this has less to do with race than it does financial status, educational level, values, and upbringing. I happen to work with several blacks, a few persons of Spanish and Mexican decent, and several of Indian and Middle-Eastern blood lines. Backgrounds and culture may differ, but people are people, no matter the color. One thing I truly believe that white supremacist groups have had wrong all along, because they are too shortsighted to see more than five feet in front of them, is believing we (whites) are the "chosen" race in any way shape or form. These clowns get things from the Bible twisted as bad as the Muslim extremists do from misreading the Qu'ran. These groups always quote the Bible, praise Jesus Christ, and claim to be the "chosen race" in God's eyes. I may not know everything, but I do know that Jesus was a Jew, and he was very likely walking the Earth in the body of an Arab man. Were the blacks not roaming Africa long before the white man inhabited the United Kingdom Isles?

From what I have seen, poor, white, live-off-the-government trailer trash are no different from the immigrants about whom we often complain. Being born in the USA does not entitle you to anything more than US citizenship. This distinction does not make you better than everyone else on the planet, and most certainly does not entitle you to a free ride on us taxpayers. Get a job, any job! Nothing is beneath you, especially if you did not finish high school, and have not attained a skilled, marketable trade of some sort. Therefore, making nine dollars per hour at Wal-Mart or Taco Bell is not an insult. People in countries like Germany, France, Poland, and Italy are not ashamed to be waiting tables, driving a cab, cleaning a hotel room, or sweeping up streets. They have to make a living, feed themselves and their children, so they "man up" and do it. They do not complain nearly as often as the "very special", lower-class, "born in the USA" person does. As far as I am concerned, there are very few legitimate ways to claim living off the tax-payers' dollar. Firstly, you served this country in the armed forces honorably, and were injured (mentally or physically) in a legitimate manner. Secondly, you are elderly, worked for many years, paid your taxes, and contributed in a positive manner, and your younger family members cannot afford to pay for your housing, medications, medical bills, etc. In this scenario, folks deserve discounted rates on necessities, fitted to what they can afford on their fixed income. Thirdly, there should be a few hundred million bucks set aside for those very special, smart, talented, young folks who can really contribute to some of our many problems here in the US. This would be in the form of grants, and the people would really have input in making them. We have gotten away from what is important, created too many loopholes (damn lawyers again), and made far too many exceptions to what should be hard, common sense, easy-to-understand rules. Coming to American from another country *should not* entitle anyone to special tax breaks, grants, interest-free loans, or longer periods to pay said loans back. Those folks should have to live by the same rules as those of us born here do. Not speaking English, having a different-color skin, and carrying a green card should never garner special treatment. The US lawmakers have really dropped the ball over the years on this one, creating more hostile attitudes toward minorities in my view.

Once again, regardless of your skin color, you should work for it, live by the same laws, and be given no special breaks. The slavery years occurred over a hundred years before any of us were born. A handful of men brought Africans over on ships and used them as slave labor. That is unfortunate, inhumane, and wrong on every level. With that being said, we have too many other issues to address in the current time frame to be worried about giving the great, great, great, great grandchildren of slaves large checks for simply being related to these men and women of 150 years ago. Using this logic, since my last name is Kaiser and that word literally means "king or ruler" in German, I would then be entitled to a percentage of the fortunes of past rulers in Deutschland, simply because of my last name. All of us, including blacks and Hispanics, need to work for it. Things can be simplified if we stick to common-sense rules. Basically, if you are not severely physically ill, mentally ill, or physically handicapped, you can work, so get out there and do so.

Racism is certainly not a thing of the past, but you get the feeling we have moved beyond it being a major dilemma in many areas. The recent financial crisis, housing crises, Hurricane Katrina, and other events have brought people of all races together. Some of the fundraising for such events has been very impressive.

Chapter 8
Pregnancy for Dummies

The liberals will have us believe that all human beings are special, deserve a chance, and someone needs to pay for them. I know this is a tough, hard-nosed approach to take, but I stand by the following statements:

Having a baby is very expensive. The costs of the birth alone, even if that birth is normal and complication-free, remains very costly. We're not even getting into the costs involved after the baby is born. Diapers, clothing, formula, and meds are very expensive. It is almost 2009, people, so being young and ignorant is not a valid excuse. Lying down with the first boy who comes along because you think it's "true love" is not an excuse. If you cannot afford to have a baby financially, mentally, or any other way, *do not get pregnant!* I cannot say it any more clearly than that.

If you do become pregnant, cannot pay for any of the costs, and in your mind abortion is "not an option due to my religious beliefs," then get a second and third job to pay for this child. We take no responsibility. In what twisted sense of accountability are taxpayers responsible for teens getting pregnant with neither of the parents bringing in a dime? What color is the sky in the world of uneducated crack whores, hillbillies, and halfwits who think it is their birth rights to have babies on complete strangers' tabs? The "share-the-wealth" crap does not work here either. Silly me,

I waited until I had a home with equity, a decent amount of money in the bank, some other assets, a college education, and a steady income over fifty thousand dollars per year before I had a child of my own. I must not have gotten the same memo my step daughter and many other folks received that says, "Hey, just have a baby and see what happens. Do not worry about the cost—the idiot tax payers have got it!"

This again speaks to earlier statements about accountability, common sense, and making no excuses. Think with your head first, not your groin area and hormones, people! We have dug ourselves such a deep financial hole by giving people a free ride we will never be able to get out. Parents have to be tougher on their teens as far as this is concerned. Anyone can make one mistake. If we limit ourselves to one, learn from it, and do not do it again—that is being a responsible human being. For poor women to keep bringing children into the world, over and over again, at the expense of you and me…It has to stop. The estimated cost of raising a child to the age of eighteen has hit as high as four hundred thousand dollars. This is if you do so properly and give that child everything he or she needs. If we are staring at two hundred babies born out of wedlock to penniless teens, street walkers, and the homeless, where does it end? How can a couple who won't earn four hundred thousand in their lifetime have five children? Do the math; it does not work.

You want solutions, as do we all. I say we have to take the hard line on this issue as well if we ever want things to improve. Parents have to be accountable. Usually they are when young teens get pregnant, but we simply cannot allow it to happen a *second* time. Make your daughter get on birth control, monitor it, and lay down serious, very real consequences if they get pregnant a second time before they are prepared. Living at home with Mommy and Daddy, regardless of the size of your home, how many cars your parents may have parked in the driveway, and how roomy your bedroom may be, is not the same thing as being prepared to care for the child properly, young ladies. Young boys and men will say anything and do anything to get into your pants, so remember that please. They even go as far as making excuses for not wearing a condom. Girls should not being having sex at such young ages as it is, but if you choose to do so, "No condom, no sex" simply has to be the rule. Everybody wins that way. Disease and pregnancy at the age of fifteen or sixteen is not a way to start your life. Not only will you being paying for this for the next twenty to twenty-five years, so will the tax payers. Animals have an excuse for breeding more offspring than they can care for; people do not.

This is simply another area where we have to be better at education and prevention. How can we seriously address issues like the environment, offshore drilling, and being green when we cannot control our population and spending? I happen to love children, and I am very comfortable around them. I consider them gifts from above, and wish for each and every child to have everything he or she needs to make it in this world. That is precisely why I feel it is so very important to bring a child into the world only in the proper environment. We have allowed everything to be skewed and distorted, twisting freedom into a modern day Sodom and Gomorra. Whether or not you believe in God or a higher power, it simply cannot be denied that females were intended to give birth, and males were intended to provide the sperm for her eggs. This the cycle of life, and there simply is no debate. Mother Nature's obvious design was for a man to insert his organ into a woman. This brings both pleasure and a good chance of conception. There is no argument that makes any sense when it comes to creating life. Sexual intercourse was not intended take place between members of the same sex. We have gotten that horribly twisted over the years.

No matter the higher power you choose to believe in, there can be no argument that male on male organs and female on female organs can result in birth among human beings. Since this is so obviously the case, why do we even waste time with gay rights and marriage cases in our courts? Answer: The liberals always confuse the laws of man with the laws of God and human nature. *Hey, if Tom wants to have sex with Harry, and Jane wants to do likewise with Sarah, so be it.* Most people have no problem with such relationships, so long as they are not flaunted publicly. Quit being so me, me, me, look at selfish little ole me all the time! Being gay does not qualify you for special rights, treatment, or arrangements in our society. Homosexual activity has gone on since the beginning of time, but recognizing two members of the same sex as a married couple is not progress. It helps nobody in particular. The argument that you have so much love to give an adopted child does not hold water either. A very young child needs a fighting chance at life. He or she does not need the confusion of the gay lifestyle the same week they are learning about where babies actually come from in school. How would you answer this question from a seven year old: "But Daddy, you and my other daddy have sex in the butt. Is this not how it is supposed to be? I am confused now." The teacher tells them sex should only be between a man and a woman and take place only after you are married adults. Whether you believe in this concept or not is not the important thing. Stop being selfish and let the child fit into normal society and see what the majority of folks believe in. If he or she chooses a different lifestyle later in life, that is fine. It is not for you to push your gay lifestyle upon an adopted child, so this kind of scenario should not be allowed to happen. Keep the gay stuff to yourselves, and quit wasting tax-payer dollars on police overtime, court costs, and many other expenses because you are so selfish, insecure, and lost in your own gay world. The fact is, California may be the most left wing, liberal, hippie, beatnik place on the planet. If an overwhelming two-thirds of that state believe that marriage and raising children is definitely reserved for one man, one woman, and they still do, give it up. You have no chance in this lifetime or the next. Only in Marin County, or perhaps South Beach in Miami, Florida will there be enough insider gay influence to make a difference on a local level. Of the three hundred billion people in America, over two hundred billion (easily) still have core values that will indeed protect the children regardless of what the gay folks think. With that in mind, again, please keep it to yourselves. This is a battle you will not win, and it's not going to change soon.

Besides, many of us are beginning to wonder if gay folks work. Each time I turn on CNN or Fox News and see protests about such silly things, it appears to be taking place during the morning or afternoon, and done so on a weekday. What, no job to keep you busy on a Wednesday morning? Oh, sorry, you must be collecting permanent disability on my dime.

Education is the key. It seems we need to take drastic measures, such as forced birth control in places like Africa, India, and South America and Asia. Religious beliefs, left- and right-type arguments, and bantering back and forth is not going to feed the millions of starving children. Talking about till we are blue in the face it will not stop the horrible disease crises in third-world countries. When the resources run out, what will you say then? In places like India, they smartest people on the planet are running out of ways to keep the water supplies drinkable, and supply its people with medicine and food. They are having a real issue with fecal matter in the water supplies causing more disease. There are simply too many people, not enough resources. This problem has to be cut off at the source. It makes no sense on any level for a disease-ridden woman with no money and living in a shack next to a pile of garbage to have twelve children. However, that is the uneducated, twisted logic of many of these women in such places. They believe that 90 percent of their children will die of starvation and disease, so they have 12 to 15, hoping 1 or 2 will actually make it. I cannot even respond to that logic, but I have seen and heard this in the translator's words. I am simply dumbfounded by this one.

People in the free world can knock the communists all they want, but the Chinese government may have had no choice in restricting the number of children its couples could birth. They may not have gone about it exactly the right way, from a human-rights point of view, but something had to be done. There are simply too many people, not enough resources. We have similar issues in America, and things will not get better in the foreseeable future. While we may not have to worry about space, water supplies, food and medicine running out tomorrow, we do have issues to be sure. We simply cannot continue to enable or even reward young, indigent girls and drug addicts to bring children into a world down in the count already. It is not fair to the taxpayers to have to foot the bill for this kind of thing. I think we have done a reasonably good job with Planned Parenthood seminars, STD classes, and other educational courses at the junior high- and high-school levels over the past twenty years. Teen pregnancies were down just about every year for quite some time but have gotten out of control again the past two years for some reason. We must do more to educate these young folks, and it needs to be done right now. In my view, we need to make the young people understand the cost of birthing, raising, and caring for each and every child. If they are made to believe that the taxpayers will no longer pay for anything and that their child will be taken from them if they cannot pay for all things the child needs, word will spread quickly. Allowing them access to so many government-assistance programs, giving them such a large financial crutch from parents, and simply enabling the entire process has gotten us into trouble. One of the most sickening things I have read about in my entire life was this recent "get-pregnant" pact by these teen girls at a high school in the Northeast US. It seems fifteen to eighteen girls agreed to get back at their parents and society by having unprotected sex with strangers, homeless guys, and other males in the town. The message that should have been sent to these girls by each and every parent is simple. *Get out of my house, I raised you better than this!* The state should have then taken each and every child away and put them up for adoption immediately after birth. While you're at it, sew these young girls up, because they are far too dumb to be a mother.

This may seem harsh, but we need tough love and hard, fast rules on such matters. Somehow, these fifteen or so gals had no clue at all about life. Somehow they were so wrapped up in their fantasy worlds that they gave no consideration to their own families, the taxpayers (I am quite certain many of them applied for assistance), their community, and, most importantly, the young life they were bringing into the world. How many of them contracted an STD of some sort? If indeed they were this ignorant and irresponsible on purpose, as a group, they should be punished as so. These girls should all be given a tab and made to pay back each and every dime to their parents, grandparents, taxpayers, and community. I would even go so far as to make them work full time and take every cent of their pay until the tab is paid in full—then they would be required to go back and graduate from school. Then and only then, could they be granted custody of their bastard children. Ignorance is not an excuse anymore. We are supposed to be the most advanced, educated, wealthy, technologically skilled, healthiest nation on the planet, so let's start acting like it. We are not any of those things at the moment, but we could and should be all of the above. We have no excuses other than laziness, lack of preparation, and a I-did-not-know-any-better attitude, which applies to all races, creeds, religions, and classes. We can do better; we just need to apply ourselves and stop expecting something for nothing.

Having children for whom you cannot care and letting the local, state, and federal governments pay for them is setting your child up for failure. Bottom line: If you cannot afford to have a child, do not have one. If you have no place for them to live, don't get knocked up! If you cannot provide health insurance for the child and are expecting someone else to foot the bill, wrong answer! Move you lazy butt to Canada! Being politically correct and walking on religious egg shells because we are so afraid to offend someone has failed miserably. If that is the truth, not perception, it is fact on so many levels that we need to stop whining and cow-towing to everyone. Let's tell our young ones how it is, pull no punches, and make them pay with real consequences when they make big mistakes. Small mistakes, errors, snafus, and hiccups are a natural thing for human beings. They are especially natural and expected amongst our young people. Getting pregnant and passing around STDs to half the neighborhood is a very large mistake, not a little booboo, so it is imperative that we prevent it from happening. More importantly, starting a newborn off so far behind in the count is setting us all up for failure on the big playing field over the long haul. This kind of thing is a mindset and general way of thinking amongst us, and it is spreading like cancer. If a young mom has a child out of wedlock, goes back home to her parents' trailer, collects a government check for year, never has to actually pay for formula, health care, diapers, and other necessities out of her own pocket, what do you think happens? It goes on and on for generations because they pretend to not know any better. It is our job on a national level to educate better. This can definitely be done if we stop wasting so much taxpayer money on taking care of the children of the young parents who cannot do it themselves, then give that money to our teachers. I am all for a flat tax that eliminates government programs and oversight committees, etc. Take that wasted pile of billions and billions, then start paying our teachers much better base salaries, then reward them with fat bonuses when their students succeed in the classroom, and move on to college, etc. Paying for performance, I think I have heard that one before. This kind of incentive is guaranteed to bring more of our best and brightest into teaching, and they will make it their personal quests to keep our children off the streets, out of the birthing centers & venereal disease clinics, and focused on becoming productive adults at all costs.

This kind of mindset will then become a fifty, perhaps one-hundred-year trend. We must take these steps and do so now, because the general feeling is that we are becoming dangerously close to forgetting how to be self-sufficient as a nation. Again, we have no excuse for such a mentality. We have the knowledge, resources, and foundation in America to do much better in this area.

Chapter 9
Why the World's Police Force?

Over the past one hundred years or so, the United States has certainly stuck her big nose into her fair share of messes in faraway lands. It would be an impossible task to even begin to try to account for the many billions and billions we have poured in to conflicts and political issues far away from US soil. The geniuses on Capital Hill have seen to it that Lady Liberty must be considered the world's policeman, private security guard, and arbitrator. This mindset in Washington has done nothing more than deepen the hatred for American around the world. Basically, we have spent many billions in taxpayer dollars on temporary bandages, duct tape, and lots of weapons. What has this resolved? Not much in the overall scheme of things. Many American lives have been lost in places like Somalia, Afghanistan, and Iraq with very little in the way of results.

How many times have we poured hundreds of millions of dollars into a foreign country, only to have them thumb their collective noses at us at the very next NATO, United Nations, or Great Eight meeting? The answer is probably too many to tally up. The problem is very simple to break down, but far too complicated to repair over night. The Washington old timers and schmoozers are unfortunately too firmly entrenched in their leather chairs to be moved any time soon. I've got news for you; politics has nothing to do with what the majority wants. Political figures over the past one hundred years obviously do not have to score highly on common-sense or foreign-relations exams. These folks are very free with our tax dollars, getting involved in a seemingly endless myriad of messes in countries of which the average American has not heard and about which certainly does not care. Politicians find it necessary to flex their money and military might in places that many of us dumb ole civilians just ain't got the real smarts to understand, or so they think.

Anyone who thinks the ongoing war in Iraq was waged for any other reason outside President Bush having a personal vendetta against the Saddam Hussein & his two sons may be living in a fantasy land. Mr. Bush had intelligence linking Saddam and his closest personal henchmen to a failed hit on his daddy, Bush Sr. several years ago. That was all the excuse he needed to send over four thousand GIs and Marines to their deaths. Political nitwits have put several spins on the war, but none of them have any real substance or weight behind them. Saving a dime or two on a gallon of gas was the second reason, but they could not come up with anything more to fool even the most patriotic citizen into believing this was a necessary war. Naming this mess "Operation Iraqi Freedom" is a slap in the face to anyone who has the ability to form a free thought. I served honorably in the United States Army in the mideighties, and will always stand behind our troops, no matter the fight or conflict. They are following orders, laying their lives on the line so you and I do not have to. That is their job, and they do it very well. War is nothing more than a political tool to show power. Are we achieving a real goal in Iraq or Afghanistan? Not one that I can clearly see. They can spin this anyway they want, but there never was a real threat to American soil. With that in mind, trying to justify the billions and billions of dollars spent, thousands of lives sacrificed, and friendships in foreign lands shattered is ludicrous. Obviously, there is a state of lawlessness in Afghanistan, and terrorists have been training there for many years. Someone has to do something about it, and the US has indeed made an impact. However, until we get some real cooperation from bordering countries, which may never occur, this kind of thing will never truly be stopped. Pakistan has been a hotbed of terror activity, their government not able or willing to do much about it.

On one hand, we do have to try to make a difference in such nasty places. However, I am convinced politicians and high-ranking military officials are no longer in touch with reality when it comes to spending our money. They budget in the billions, throwing our money at problems, which are indeed real money pits. Until they are held personally accountable, nothing will change. After all, it is not their money. Until senators, generals, and house representatives see their personal bank accounts and assets being affected, nothing will change. They will continue to toss our money down any black hole they see fit.

Tax dollars were never supposed to be so carelessly flaunted and wasted by the millions and billions. The political machine in Washington, DC has gotten so careless with tax dollars, recovery in several lifetimes may not be a realistic goal. That concerns me, as it does anyone with children and grandchildren for whom they care about. Unfortunately, we the people no longer have an intimate, working relationship with any of the folks on Capital Hill. They are very much out of touch with what the average American needs, and we only see or hear from them when they are front-page news due to the latest crime or scandal in which one or more of our elected officials are involved. Taking care of problems on the other side of the planet has been a priority for Congress for many years. In my view, a country should learn to properly police itself before doing so abroad. We have not learned how to police and control our government officials effectively. They have a blank check for almost anything without the proper checks and balances in place.

Quite simply put, we need to finish the job when we commit so many millions and billions of dollars abroad. Whether it be the conflict in Vietnam, Korea, Somalia, or Iraq I and II, we are not getting positive results. Throwing money and military might around has long been the way of doing things in Washington, but it has not worked. We are facing a very real crisis here on US soil, so we need all our resources focused on fixing our own country. Getting out of Iraq as soon as we can do so safely must be a priority. Choosing to ignore the crises in Africa, the Middle

East, and other places around the world is indeed a tough decision, but one that we have to make for the near future. Any and all resources must be applied here at home, and done so in a common-sense, feasible manner. It makes no sense at all to think we can stabilize situations in faraway lands when things are far from stable here at home. Before we stick our nose and our wallet into foreign messes, let's try something new here in America. How about we get a handle on our auto industry, financial nightmare, and educational issues, just for starters? Would that be okay? Perhaps when those things are repaired, say in 2055, we can think about spending another five hundred billion dollars and sacrificing an additional five thousand young lives on something as silly as oil or a personal vendetta.

Chapter 10
All Right, How Can We Fix Things?

We have already established that the financial heart of America is broken in many ways. How can things get fixed in a timely manner? For starters, we must not waste time finger-pointing, laying blame, and spending millions trying to find out who, what, where, why, and how things got so bad on Wall Street, in Detroit, and on Capital Hill. Bickering and arguing will also waste precious time we do not really have. Let's do everything we can to repair things now, then worry about who is to blame later. America needs everyone, and I mean everyone to come together on the same page in order to focus our attention correctly. We need our smartest, richest, most powerful men and women to chip in with their time, money, and ideas to avoid a complete collapse. We are indeed competing in a global economy now, but that global machine gets most of its juice right here in the good ole US of A.

When I say that everyone needs to chip in, I mean just that. My family is very much stuck in the middle of the middle class from a financial standpoint. We generally get a modest tax return of $1,200 to $2,500 each year. Personally, if I know for a fact that it would help matters, the IRS can keep that money and put it to good use towards our nation's recovery. We need new ideas. We simply must save the auto industry, despite the very much avoidable mistakes they have made to put themselves into this disastrous mess. We have to take immediate action to save hundreds of thousands of jobs because the late-2008 job numbers clearly show we are in a recession. It is not the right time to allow such an important, large, vital industry to fail. The people at the top of GM, Chrysler, and Ford have badly mismanaged things. However, the parts suppliers, dealerships, UAW, and white-collar folks will all have to make very real concessions right now. It cannot wait three to six months. I still believe that simply printing more money, tacking it onto the federal deficit, and worrying about how we can generate enough to pay it back later is not the right way to do things. With that in mind, we have got to come up with some cash to pay for this bailout/loan/handout for the automakers. This is not the textbook way to recover. This is not the way things were supposed to be, but they are. Drastic times call for drastic measures, and we are knee-deep into a world financial crisis. That crisis was started and fueled right here in America. The Wall Street crooks are even more to blame than the morons in Motown, but we cannot focus time and money on that at this very moment. We must make America strong again as soon as we possibly can.

These are indeed just words. I am not pointing in a real direction you say? There are three hundred million people in American. At least a third of those folks are not poor or struggling. It's time to make real contributions to save our country. We have to come together as one like we did during World War II. People have to give up the finer things in life—the luxuries, if you will—if only for a year or two. This will make a huge dent in our debt. Everyone needs to do without pampering themselves for a while to save a country that is definitely worth saving. It starts small, but in very important ways. Firstly, we need to think of the bigger picture, and not be so wrapped up in our little yuppie worlds. That twelve year old with a cell phone he or she does not need—get rid of his or her phone. If you normally cheat just a little on your tax return to break even, or get just a little back, stop it for a few years. Pay your taxes on time and in full. If you are one of the one hundred million Americans of whom I speak who have just a little more than they need, you'll have to think of others first. Let's make the little sacrifices together, as it is the only way.

The guys in Washington simply must set the example, and do so where the public can see them. For the time being, no more lunches at Ruth's Chris or Morton's on the taxpayers' dime. No more nine-hundred-dollar suits and two-hundred-and-fifty-dollar shoes. You can shop at Men's Warehouse or JC Penney for a two-hundred-dollar suit just like the rest of us. No more limo rides, helicopter trips to the airport, or unnecessary motorcades. Each and every member of the Senate and Congress needs to cut his or her expenditures by 50 percent, and the salaries by at least 10 percent, for starters. If they do this, it will send a strong message to the upper and middle class to act. It is not going to kill these folks to eat lunch at a DC deli for eight dollars for at least four days per week. You and I can likely get by without the four-dollar daily latte from Starbucks. If those of us who are in the middle of that one hundred million of whom I speak are willing, myself included, we can do it. Personally, I have no problem with taking the twenty-five dollars per week I spend at my local watering hole and giving it directly to Detroit. If you folks who chat for fifteen hundred minutes on the cell each month about absolutely nothing could get over that silly habit, especially while you're in the car, perhaps cut down to a five-hundred-minute minute plan, this would save you at least twenty dollars per month. Apply that money to the solution. The aforementioned daily coffee drinkers could take the five or even ten dollars per day and give 80 percent of it toward a real solution. You can survive on a $1.25 cup of Maxwell House coffee for a while. Personally, I travel frequently and stay in four- and five-star hotels almost each and every trip. Certainly, I can make it for a couple of years at the Holiday Inn at one hundred dollars per night instead of the four hundred dollars I have spent many times elsewhere. Tell me where to sign, and to whom to give the money.

For those of you who like to gamble, the true art of burning money, you can help a great deal. Casinos need hundreds of employees and large, sophisticated machines to count all the money they take in on a daily basis. That means you are not winning, despite what you tell the wife and your friends. Get over the habit for a year or two and send some of this wasted money to where it's needed most. You will feel much better about giving your money away in this manner, I promise you. Businesses have to cut out 401K matches and a great deal of their company travel for a while. Sacrifices have to be real and affect our bottom line right away.

For those of you who happen to be devout Christians, attending your local church each and every Sunday, you can help, too. Instead of putting a bit over the 10 percent tithe rule, giving 15 percent or more like you normally do, stick to 10 percent for awhile. That money can possibly help save jobs and save the American way of life.

We are not strangers, but on the same team here, people. There happens to be a large percentage of people in this country who eat out three or four nights per week. Cut that down to one night and purchase some basic, inexpensive dinners at the grocery store. That could easily be one hundred dollars per week right there. Buy savings bonds or CDs with it and donate where needed. The big problem is finding the right people to distribute the money. Since everything is done electronically these days, a handful of government people release these large sums of money to the banks. From there, it is anyone's guess as to where it goes, and to whom it goes. Funds that are intended to get directly into the hands of small businesses and neighborhoods are being spent on past debt and mistakes. This kind of thing is just too complex, and there are too many chiefs and not enough Indians working on the distribution of the money.

The only way to fix this is for each and every one of us to start using the less selfish side of our brains. Bankers and lenders need to get this money where it is needed most, and do so quickly. The Wall Street crooks have clearly shown us that they do not know how to manage their own money very well, and cannot be trusted. Without integrity, trust, and a sense of urgency, there is no way we will return to the world's clear-cut economic power. What these guys at Lehman Bros. and other such firms have done is make it nearly impossible for the straight shooters on Wall Street and in other sectors of the financial and investment world to ever be trusted again. Selfishness, weakness, poor business training and etiquette, and outright terrible decision making by these baboons at the top have made the financial foundation of future generations in this country nearly impossible to restore. My daughter is a senior in high school and has talked openly with me about wanting to be a corporate accountant many times. While dousing a child's dreams is not an easy thing to do, I have recently been brutally honest with her. I told her that accounting at the corporate and big-business level may never again be looked upon positively, or at least not in our lifetime. The average person around the world for this generation and the next will always assume that bean counters at big companies in America are "cooking the books" and inflating their stock illegally. That's a shame, because there are many good firms that do things the right way.

The new mentality at the top of these Fortune 1000 companies simply has to be "We will get caught if we cheat" from this point forward. We would be better served is each and every one of these CEOs and CFOs enough had backbone, integrity, and sense of responsibility to the entire nation to do things right because it's the right thing to do. However, man is and always has been driven by personal greed, so we will have to take baby steps the first ten years or so in hopes these guys will just do a better job because they have to do a better job. It is a no-brainer in my humble opinion that corporate big wigs need incentive-laden contracts only. Guaranteed money, stock options, toys, homes, cars, country club memberships, and other perks should be given based on performance. If you are one of the ten or twelve people in charge, your performance is based on what the entire company is doing. Getting twenty million on the way out the door after the stock falls 35 percent is ludicrous. From this point forward, anyone and everyone sitting on a board of directors at GM, Ford, Chrysler, Merrill-Lynch, Prudential, GE, or any other company should consider it an act of lunacy to sign off on a contract that rewards anything less than total success. A mediocre or bad job over a two-or-three-year span can no longer be rewarded with one hundred thousand shares of company stock, a million-dollar home, and a fifteen-million-dollar "golden parachute" clause of any kind. If they do sign off on such a bad idea, fire them immediately. We cannot succeed and once again get to the forefront of the financial world if we reward people for subpar performance. It really is as simple as that. If the stock does not rise, and the companies' true (not creatively spun by accountants) bottom lines does not improve by such and such percent, newly appointed CEO, CFO, or CIO Fred Jones gets nothing other than a pink slip. If you do well, you will reap the rewards. If not, you should never become richer.

This is the part where corporate snobs and seven-figure guys and gals who have never known even a middle-class lifestyle, much less what it is like to struggle, might say, "It's not that simple; things are more complex than that," etc. Yes, it is that simple, you pompous fool! If the company is not making a real profit, you get only your base salary, no bonuses or stocks. If the company does poorly three years consecutively, you get the door. It is truly that simple. And one more thing, we do understand it, and it is not that complex. Over the past thirty or forty years, inflating the stock and selling shares was all that mattered. Actually having cash and real assets was nowhere near the top of the list of priorities for these corporate hotshots. The only way we fix this mess is for everyone to be accountable all the time, and for these people to stop hiding behind smoke-and-mirror BS. like "company security measures" and government restrictions. It should not matter that Sally Smith did a great job at Xerox, turning the company around in just four years. While it is impressive that she took the company from five billion in debt to five hundred million into the black in just the past eight quarters, streamlining costs, and returning the confidence to their customer base—that does not mean she can fix Chrysler. Dangling guaranteed money in front of her to lure her to Chrysler makes no sense. Everyone has to want to be there for something more than a fat paycheck and stock war chest. The people on the top floor in Troy, Michigan must really want the company to succeed and not expect something for nothing. The same goes for the middle-management level advertising guy, the dealership GM, and the shift foreman/leader on nights at the assembly plant. Pointing the collective finger at the union deals signed thirty years ago and healthcare costs is not acceptable. Everyone has to concede and give up something real to make this work. Sally Smith gets richer only if things are truly returned to profitability, and the taxpayers get some of their money back within five years. You do not need a one thousand page contract, and a room full of lawyers getting five hundred dollars per hour for this stuff.

General Motors sold the same amount of automobiles in 2007 as Toyota did. One made seven billion in profits, the other lost billions. Can you guess which one lost money and why? GM can point to very poor management, too much spending, and not being able to compete in what is now a truly global marketplace. The people on the top floor of the RenCen in downtown Detroit will tell you it's too complicated and not nearly as clearcut as we (the uninformed public) think it is. They will point to the UAW contracts, operating costs, healthcare and pension costs, etc. It is very difficult to dispute the fact that those things are hurting GM in a very big way. However, the demand for cars is high, and sales are good. That should be your one and only bargaining chip when you sit down with the union representatives. You lay it out for them in simple terms.

A.   Toyota is making a car for this much. It costs GM nearly twice as much to make a similar car. They are killing us on labor, benefits, etc.

B.   Toyota, Nissan, BMW, and others sell millions of cars in the US, so we cannot survive without competing directly against them and winning.

How can things be fixed in Detroit over the next few years? Can it actually be done?

Without a company, the union folks get nothing. No jobs, zero money, no health care or pension. The workers get zip, zilch, nada. Therefore, considering sales are okay, but costs are too high, we must cut costs to stay in business. Salaried workers and execs are making too much money. Part suppliers are charging too much money. Hourly workers are getting more than you can afford to pay them in wages and benefits. To stay alive, you have to make drastic cost cuts in all of the aforementioned areas and more. The way I see it, the UAW has nothing to bargain with here. Without money to pay the workers, everyone gets nothing. Health benefits will have to be cut, only offering the most cost-effective HMO plans to full-time employees with more than one year of service. There's a start folks. Job banks and "almost-full" pay during shutdown periods are ludicrous to begin with. If you are not actually working and being productive, you get no paycheck. For the next three years, assuming the bailout package comes within the next thirty days, allowing GM and Chrysler to stay afloat, other concessions will have to be made out of sheer necessity. No overtime, period. No bonuses or stock options for anyone, period. Costs have to be brought to a minimum right now, and each car must bring some kind of profit to be applied directly toward necessary operating costs and outstanding debt. No dental plans, vision plans, no first-class travel or five-star hotels over the next three years. Unless absolutely necessary, travel abroad will have to be cut for a while.

These guys need to tear up the current union contracts and start over right now. Forget about being prideful and doing things "your way," because your way has not worked at all. You have failed miserably, so at the very least, we need to mirror the profitable and successful business model of carmakers like Toyota. To stay in business, the big three will have to match costs right down the line in each and every area with Toyota and other competitors, until restored to profitability. I can guarantee you 95 percent of the employees will choose keeping their jobs for the next couple of years over being fired, even if that means giving up 33 percent of their pay and benefits. The last resort should be touching the pensions of the retired workers. However, the airline industry had to do it, so it may have to be done to stay alive. I can also guarantee that a sixty-year-old retired man or woman will gladly give up 10 percent of their pension checks and all of their health care they are receiving instead of losing all of it. Large cuts and sacrifices on the part of everyone simply must be made in order to keep the lines operating. Any unused real estate or other unnecessary investments most be sold ASAP, even if that means taking a bit less than things may be worth. This is a crisis situation, so a "slash and burn" mindset must prevail. Even the seemingly little things like paying for lunch while sitting down with the unions will have to be cut for awhile. You guys will simply have to brown bag it.

The big three automakers are not making bad cars and trucks. This is not the issue, despite what many folks are saying. Did the executives and engineers drop the ball in a big, big way by making huge, gas-guzzling SUVs for so many years? Yes. Is the Toyota Camry a better value for the money than a Chevy mid-sized vehicle? The answer is also yes. However, we can be assured of one thing. Those men and women on the lines in Motown are doing the best job they can do, and they do take pride in their work. They do not cut corners, and have made some pretty darn good cars in recent years. Making Ford Excursions, stretch Cadillac Escalades, and GMC Suburban vehicles as a top priority was a mistake, but they must learn from that and move forward. Bottom line: Ford, GM, and, Chrysler must make cars and trucks for the same cost or less than Toyota can make the same vehicles. That is the only way to compete in a global market.

We all wish there were an easy fix for this mess. That will not be the case, as the automakers and Wall Street fat cats have dug such a huge hole. Any solution will take a very coordinated, well executed plan with plenty of concessions on all sides. When it is all said and done, the Big Three may have to become the Humongous One in order to survive. Personally, I can envision a large MMA (Michigan Motors Association) logo on the top of a newly leased building in Motown after they merge and sell off the others. Whatever it takes, we are at a crossroads here in the US. Let's take the smart route together.

Chapter 11
Get Over Yourself Already

We are so fortunate to be living in the "land of the lawyers" time. Insert sarcasm here if you so please. Modern-day Americans have become the largest bunch of whining, self-centered, oblivious to the rest of the planet group of people in the history of the world. Our courts are filled with thousands of pending cases filed for what amounts to nothing more than name calling. There are thousands more filed under "irreconcilable differences" in divorce courts across the land. Even more still lined up for people looking to collect a check for nothing more than their own incompetence, laziness, and underachieving ways. Why is this allowed? Why is this even possible? Because we are living in what was once the "Land of the Free and Home of the Brave," but now we should rename it to the "Land of the Many Lawyers and Home of the Want Something for Nothing." The United States has more personal injury attorneys than any other country has criminal defense, immigration law, real estate, and divorce attorneys combined. We have more divorce and malpractice lawyers walking around with briefcases full of ridiculous case files than any ten countries in Europe combined. Worse yet, we have a slew of clowns tying up the Judicial system with "slander" and "defamation of character" lawsuits pending from LA to Bangor, Maine. To be perfectly honest, I am tired of trying to defend the USA when I travel abroad. In the age of cable and satellite TV and almost unlimited news and gossip channels, everyone gets to see how silly we really are. I wish they could not see how embarrassingly self-centered and whiny we have become.

The past couple of generations here in my country have slid into a huge rut. So many of us think the world revolves around us. If you get into a conversation at a pub or restaurant about something not going quite right in your life, there will almost certainly be a business card or two flopped into your hand from an attorney. He or she will say, "Give me a call—we can get you some money for your pain and suffering," for sure. Only in America can those words be uttered with the confidence that Mr. or Mrs. Snooty P. Lawyer can actually bring some of this nonsense to court and win. We have become the "land of the too free" as far as filing lawsuits in concerned. People in America with any connection to the public eye have a chip on their shoulders, and perhaps something to prove to themselves. They tend to hire a lawyer for almost anything, at the drop of a hat. Do we really need a team of lawyers, publicists, agents, and other flunkies for middle-of-the-road celebrities? Hell no! Any time a silly story comes out in a magazine or paper or any other rich or famous person calls another a name, there will be one hundred ambulance chasers lined up to sue someone. We are so blind that we cannot even see how weak this has made us as a nation. People in America no longer want to work hard for anything. Instead, we muddle around in mediocrity and failure for ten or twenty years, then hire an attorney to get us a quick fix from someone rich and successful. Is this done out of spite, jealousy, laziness, or a combination of all of them?

Perhaps, but I think a large percentage of the population's mindset is now dangerously leaning toward being financially dependent upon "Somebody else, anyone but me" these days. Human beings are creatures of habit to be sure. There was a time when hiring a lawyer meant hundreds or thousands of dollars up front, they would only consider your case if it had merit, and they were convinced the judge or jury would take the time to preside over it. Nowadays, none of that matters. Poor, lazy, uneducated people have lawyers knocking on their trailer doors with the good possibility of a handout. Judges have ruled in favor of the defendant in so many of these cases it has created an entire new generation of truly unnecessary lawyers, defendants, and frivolous lawsuits. Who can blame these people? They do not know any better and are promised boatloads of money by some guy or gal in a suit with a briefcase. Heck, they do not even need a penny up front, and will not collect unless they win the case! Shoot! Sign me up, Bubba, sounds darn good to me.

Now, all these lawyers will tell themselves that they are providing a service to folks who otherwise could not afford an attorney. They know better than that, but will never publically admit that fact. The simple fact is, most attorneys are the very definition of greed and self-righteousness, and try to spin everything to suit their own bank accounts. If they do not steal this money from Joe Blow or Acme Corporation, there are certainly a thousand more lawyers waiting in line to do so. That is my point exactly, and the biggest part of the problem. Way too many lawyers have created a culture and generation of way too many cases. Easy money for you out there, brother; let me go get it for you. It makes me sick. To bring a case into a US court for nothing more than name-calling is both ludicrous and wasteful on so many levels, it's disgusting. Basically, you are saying, "He called me a name and I do not like it. It's going to cause me some professional embarrassment, personal anguish, trauma, and a great deal of pain and suffering. Somebody please give me some money to ease my grief. I need twenty million, Your Honor,, if you please." I wish these people had a slice of dignity, and the ability to step outside themselves for a few moments so they could see just how pathetic and embarrassing this kind of thing really is.

We have gone so far past the point of no return in the US court system it is impossible to see anything in the rear view mirror. How many nimrods have the ability to approve overtime and excess funding these days? It seems like an unlimited number of such people just keep digging a deeper and deeper hole each and every year. "Heck, it's taxpayer money, Buford, go ahead and spend it all son. When we ain't got no more, you can still spend it. We'll just tack it on the state's unlimited tab." This is our mindset at the local, state, county, and federal levels. Instead of weeding out the unnecessary court cases, we just hire more court reporters, judges, bailiffs, police, and administrative folks on the taxpayer dollar to handle the bill. The waste and spending is out of hand on a catastrophic level. We spend hundreds of millions in tax money on Republican and Democratic conventions, inaugurations, and all the crap that goes with what amounts to nothing more than window dressing. America, the beautiful, has become America, "the dog and pony show."

I do not completely understand from where this superiority complex in America has come. I've got news for you America: We are not that great. We are simply not number one in a great many categories, so we should stop pretending like our collective poop does not stink. Many people in this country, famous or not, think they can use our courtrooms and media as personal ego-stroking machines. Here's a clue for you folks, and you darn sure know who you are: "Get over it. You are not all that!" Please, I am begging you folks to stop wasting valuable time and money and check you selfishness at the door for a few years. If our most powerful, influential, and talented people cannot do that, we will not succeed in repairing America. We have shown that we can come together to battle crisis situations in the recent past and this current economic and financial mess most certainly falls into that category. Petty bickering, embarrassingly idiotic lawsuits, and overall poor decision making across the land because we have become so self-centered and arrogant has been slowly killing us for years. Well, we have arrived at the edge of the cliff. Do we jump to a certain death as a nation? Or, can we get over ourselves and realize that we have a great deal of work to do just to become mediocre? I certainly hope it is the latter of the two.

Until we can create a sense of urgency, not underestimate the crisis we are facing, and fully realize that we have to put our pitiful little personal issues aside, we cannot return this country to the top. You do not need to look far to see what I am talking about. I can virtually guarantee there are frivolous lawsuits filling the dockets of almost every county in America. What we have in our court buildings is an endless pile of trash serving no purpose other than making more money for a deeper and deeper pool of bottom-feeding lawyers. These people depend on our dysfunction, weak minds, overblown egos, and selfishness to make millions each and every year. Would we not be much better off if this were not the case? Absolutely we would be better off, without question.

I am not a fool. I understand that everyone has to make a living, and most people in the world feel these issues are way beyond them, too big for any one man or woman to make a dent. So, we turn the other way and just worry about taking care of number one. That is certainly understandable, but also part of the reason we are in such deep financial trouble. If the past ten years have shown us anything at all, it is that we cannot assume things are what they seem on Wall Street. We cannot assume the guys up there are handling our money with even a slice of dignity or honesty. They have used the smoke-and-mirrors method of investing, pouring billions into pyramid schemes and other foolish schemes for many years now. Those guys counted heavily on the fact that things on Wall Street were so complicated that it would be years before anyone caught on to what was happening. By the time that happened, they'd be sitting on a beach in the Caribbean with a billion dollars each. The same goes for our court systems, as the lawyers have been able to manipulate and cloud the system to such a degree nobody really knows what is and what is not a legitimate case anymore. We sue one another for just about anything, the lawyers citing evergrowing stockpiles of cases from the previous fifty years. If we would take just 20 percent of the money wasted on frivolous lawsuits and settlements over the past twenty-five years, and send it to Detroit, the automakers could be bailed out five times over. Attorneys count on the ineptness, lack of good decision making skills, and greediness of Americans to pad their luxurious lifestyles. I say we clean up our act, make the right choices for a while, and not give them the satisfaction.

In order to fix this problem, we must change one basic thing about our system of law. Judicial boards need to start deciding with an iron fist what can or cannot be tried in our courts of law. We also need to consider cost as the number one factor in allowing these trials to go on and on for what seems like an eternity, eating tax dollars at alarming rates along the way. We desperately need tort reform in the US. I am far from a law expert, but I can tell you one thing for certain. The country as a whole would be a thousand times better off if we eliminated the slander (name calling), slip and fall (clumsiness), and ridiculous cases where one moronic roommate sues the other for 180 dollars because he or she rang up their cell phone bill, etc. More importantly, we would be much better off applying common sense to cases that are obviously about getting something for nothing simply because the law allows one to sue and there are one hundred idiot lawyers lined up to take case pro bono for you. We can do that by making the loser pay every single cent. They pay every penny of the cost after the fact. How many lawsuits would not be brought to court if the person suing had everything to lose instead of nothing?

This is all tied together when you look at it closely. Our physically fat and lazy lifestyles have manifested themselves in our courts, businesses, and financial institutions. We have gotten way too fat and lazy in many ways and must trim the fat to survive. We have become creatures of habit, sitting on our butts on the couches instead of getting out there and being proactive about our country. We just let things go as they are, never being proactive and instead reacting with arms flailing when things go badly. Everything that has gone on to get us to this low point in America has been documented. We need to not only understand it but learn from it, keep it fresh in our minds, and install a foolproof system of checks and balances. The men and women at the top are not to be trusted anymore, so we have to change our way of doing things.

It is easier to swallow false pride than real pride. So many people in our nation have big heads for no reason and need a shot-in-the-arm reality check right now. One of your competitors slammed you on national TV or radio. So what? Get over it! Stop whining like a little baby, and be big enough to beat the competition on the field of battle instead of in our courts. The United States Judicial system was never intended to be a three-ring circus, but has certainly become one. The last thing I wish to do is gripe and moan without providing any solutions. I am not the smartest guy on the planet, and I may not even be in the running in my hometown. However, we do have thousands of very smart, skilled, diversely talented folks in this country. We must get them in the right places to help America get back on her feet. Who decides this? Sometimes the answer is right in your own lap, and those people need to step up to the plate and help. They know who they are better than I do for sure. Our children's future depends upon it. Their children's future also depends on what we do over the next ten to twenty years. We must admit at the very top that our legal and financial and business practices in many instances have been very poorly run, and we must get it right from this point forward. Personally, I never trusted the clowns on Wall Street, so I never put much money into stocks. Our country is not as far gone on the corruption scale within the legal community as many others, but we are not Mother Theresa either. We can do much better, and we have no reason not to do so.

Bashing lawyers in general is not my purpose in this chapter. Many of them are needed and do an excellent job. Real-estate law and criminal law are areas in which people will always need assistance. Still, we have millions of attorneys in the dysfunction and scam-money-from-the-rich-for-no-reason business—which needs to be cleaned up in a major way. Collecting large sums of money because your feelings were hurt or you are incompetent is very wrong on many levels. Guys and gals with law degrees should have more spine than to help people get this kind of money. That, in a nutshell, is why lawyers get such a well-deserved bad rap. They are like vultures: ready to swoop in and collect money no matter the reason, so long as there is a chance to do so in court. These folks think most of us are too dumb to understand things, so they complicate them even further, creating ten times the legal paperwork. Why? Obviously, it will take many more hours at $250 per hour to get through that stuff. Somebody has to pay for Mr. and Mrs. Attorney's lap dances, boats, gambling habit, drinking habit, country club membership, and mistress' apartment. Greed and zero accountability, that's what we do well.

In very recent events, we see the governor of Illinois under fire for trying to sell the open senate seat (which was vacated by Obama) to the highest bidder. The Feds have taped conversations of this clown containing all sorts of incriminating conversations. The media covers thing story as if it is big and shocking news.

That's a laugh! When have we *not* had political figures mired in the middle of criminal investigations, scandal, and illegal activity? Come on; is it really a surprise that an Illinois political figure is dishonest and shady? This guy looks like a complete crook. He is just another in a long line of standup guys in the great state of Illinois. They have been breeding such straight shooters and inserting them into office since the 1920s, so why stop now. This kind of thing is no longer a situation where one can say "It's almost as if these guys think they are untouchable." Lawyers and political figures really believe they can do just about anything and spin their way out of it. Lie, cheat, steal, bribe, corrupt, sleep around, and whatever else it may take, baby!

Chapter 12
Just Give Them a Pill

In yet another glaring example of America's lazy supremacy over the rest of the globe, we now have forced it upon those we should be protecting, molding, nurturing, and shaping. If the past thirty or so years have shown us anything, it is that we have lost control of our children to cable and satellite TV, the internet, and cellular phones. Parents have relinquished control and discipline over their teens and preteens much too easily. In our quest for more home than we need, for more toys and automobiles than the next-door neighbor, and to pay off our credit-card debt, a large chunk of the middle class have become dual full-time income homes. In many instances, children have been unsupervised for several hours per day, five days per week. This has been a disaster waiting to happen for many years, and here we are folks. The number of homes in which both parents work full time is staggeringly higher than what it was thirty-five years ago. Moreover, one can easily see that a high number of those homes are made up of people on their second, third, and even fourth marriages. Huge numbers of broken homes, scattered siblings, and bitter divorces—just more things that we do here in America better than anyone else on the planet.

We have become so caught up in the chase for the almighty dollar, and so self centered, we no longer put the children first. This is a cycle that absolutely must stop, or we will pay an even heavier price over the next thirty years. It is simply unacceptable for us to continuously say, "Well, that's just the way it is these days; it's a different time." Not true. Before you get married and start a family, very real discussions need to take place. Children need discipline and almost constant supervision until the age of sixteen or so, whether they want it or not. This kind of thing must be in your game plan when starting a family. All of the dysfunction I have mentioned previously in the book is tied together. Those individuals raised in the past two generations have become all too familiar with being raised as young children by strangers at daycare, then passed on to a neighbor here and there in the fifth grade, and then left completely unsupervised from the age of twelve or thirteen. With technology at the forefront in recent years, we have less influence on what our kids think and believe than people did one hundred years ago. The problem is: We should know better. We have quite frankly not learned from our mistakes. America has regressed badly in this area instead of progressed.

Our smugness and superiority-over-the-rest-of-the-globe complex has hurt us badly in the global markets. The Chinese, Europeans, South Americans, and countries such as India have caught and passed us in many technological, financial, educational, and business training arenas. We used to be the best at almost everything, not any longer. Now, we just think we are the best, but do not produce the results. This kind of smugness has hurt our country from a parenting standpoint as well. Do you see where I am going with this? Everything: all our issues, problems, shortcomings, and failures in business, banking, and world trade these past thirty years or so can be tied together with our overall failures in the home and in our many school systems. We have become so afraid of lawsuits, so scared of being politically and religiously incorrect, and so worried about our own selfish images, we have forgotten what is important. We have forgotten how to use discipline, good ole fashioned hard work, and integrity in the home and at school. Instead, we bend the rules, tell our youth it's not their fault, and send them to a shrink. Soon thereafter, they might be diagnosed with ADD or ADHD, or some other fine example of our dysfunctional society and its love affair with the quick, but expensive, fix. You're telling me with a straight face, and every bit of personal confidence that you believe a stranger in an office building with a degree from Eastern Kentucky Community College has a better idea of how to control your child's behavior than you do? Just give them a pill; Sally and Jimmy have ADHD. Good enough for me. Lord knows, we would not want to apply discipline, tough love, and actually be a parent when a child cries out for such attention. It's simple folks; and I really mean simple. If your teen gets insubordinate, fails or skips class, or gets in trouble on a regular basis, you take away the things they like. No cell phone, PC, or TV in their room, and you actually make them do chores around the home for a number of weeks, until they get their grades back up. This is not rocket science or brain surgery and you do not need advice from Dr. Phil, Oprah, or Jerry Springer. If things get really out of hand, you put them in military school or on basic lockdown at the home until they comply. Giving ten, twelve, and fourteen year olds mind-altering drugs is definitely not the answer. I did not need to attend medical school or a psychology program of any kind to figure that one out.

You will see serious behavioral patterns in your child, well before they actually become serious, if your eyes are simply open. Make them go outside and burn off energy. Make them adapt to the society around them. Letting your child cloud his or her mind with the adult internet, violent video games, and constant texting back and forth to bad influences is a disaster waiting to happen. This kind of technological mess has not helped our kids one bit. They sit in school for six hours, talking to their idiot best friend, then come home and sit on their butts for another four hours, texting and instant messaging the same kids. That's ten hours a day almost completely wasted. Kids need adult interaction, conversation, fresh air, and outdoor exercise. This is Common Sense 101 and Child Raising 101, people. Also, I do not care what anyone says, and do not want to hear each and every case on an individual basis. Plain and simple, cut and dry, we have failed our kids with the cell phone thing. There is no good reason for a ten, eleven, or thirteen-year-old child to have a cell phone! Take the money you are wasting on this garbage and put it into a college fund, please. Nobody is going to tell me that a fifth grader who is either home, at school, or playing in the neighborhood actually needs a cell phone to text his fellow spoiled and lazy pal, who happens to live one hundred yards down the street. We need to stop making excuses, stop throwing gadgets at our kids just to get them out of our hairdos, and give them real, consistent structure.

Bear in mind, I have worked in information technology for the better part of twenty-two years now. The field has taught me a great deal, paid the mortgage, put bread on the table, and afforded me a few luxuries over the years. However, this is too important to pretend all is well and simply look the other way. Technology, for the most part, has not helped our children. Think about it for a few moments. The data and research are there in great quantities to back me up, and I have given this subject a great deal of thought. Children have a great amount of nervous energy and a high metabolism, and they actually require sunlight. What have we done the past twenty years or more? We give them as many technologically wonderful gadgets as we can come up with to keep them sitting indoors on their butts and getting fatter and lazier by the week. In the vast majority of the cases, the children are not getting any smarter. Any decent school in this day and age has at the very least a shared computer lab, where our kids can get time on the web, supervised, as it should be. Therefore, they do not need a cell phone, PDA, laptop, and desktop at home to use as they please. This is simply not a good environment for a young person's mind and body to grow productively. Best case scenario would have a circle of three or four friends constantly e-mailing and texting each other through the week—perhaps fifty hours or more. In today's teen environment, we may be lucky if one kid in the aforementioned small group is sharper than the average house plant. These kids bounce useless info and chit-chat off one another all day long, six or seven days per week, rarely interacting with adults or others in their respective communities for more than a few minutes here and there. Do the math. This is not a good environment for a young person's mind and personality to grow.

Technology, busy schedules, two working parents, and our lack of commitment to a solid family foundation also nearly eliminated one very important thing within the household: the family face-to-face dinner. Our teens now text us that they are grabbing a burger and fries with a friend, and we miss out on the important conversation, body language, and daily information from our kids that any good parent should desire. We were much better off as a family unit before kids were allowed to do whatever they wanted at dinner time. This kind of thing has contributed greatly to our teen obesity problems, not to mention our not actually supervising our children ten or twelve hours per day or more. We absolutely must get back to basics in the home. A ton of love, structure, confidence, and open communication will do much more for your child's future than a visit to the local quack and a few dozen pills. In my humble opinion, these clowns in the psychological field who prescribe pills that essentially turn young folks into zombies, and do so regularly—are the biggest child abusers of all. "Here you go, young man. Take this pill, give me one hundred dollars, then come back in two weeks with another one hundred dollars," and repeat. This is a tragedy, but has become all too regular in our society. Quick fixes, shuffling things under the rug, and synthetic "band-aids" are unacceptable where our precious children are concerned. They are the future, and will no doubt have to clean up many of the messes we have created. For this tall task, they need discipline, love, structure, real education, and the security blanket that comes with knowing your parents are not only competent, but in your corner all the way.

The practices of grading on curves, pushing kids through the system, and allowing them to drop certain required course material for easier classes has hurt us in a big way. Selling our already long-in-the-sarcasm-department teens on respecting adult authority and getting back to the basics will be tough, as the adults have not done a very good job in recent memory. However, this is a must do. We have to start with the children, almost as if we are building the country all over again. In a sense, we really are doing just that. Giving them a pill or a twenty-dollar bill to go away is never the answer. Let's hold one another, as parents, fully accountable for getting our kids to respect authority once again, study harder, and believe in their own futures. Without that kind of commitment, we are doomed to slip even further behind the rest of the world. While the US is still the mightiest military in the world, we have slipped badly in the areas of education from middle school through the university and graduate levels. Our standardized test scores versus China's, Japan's, Germany's, Israel's, India's, and several others' have not been good. We can do better. We must do better. Giving kids mind-altering drugs at a young age is not the answer. It needs to stop now. We may look back on TV shows like *Leave It to Beaver* and *Happy Days* with laughter. We may consider them very "corny" and goofy, but they were actually not far off from what life was really like in the 1950s here in the United States. Starting with something seemingly so simple like having our youth use proper greetings like "Good morning, sir," or "Good morning, ma'am," and saying "Yes, sir," etc.. can go a very long way. Talking back with little or no respect to authority figures cannot be thrown in to a pyschologist's category such as ADD or ADHD. This all starts with upbringing. We need to instill etiquette, manners, good study habits, and structure long before we start rewarding kids for doing little more than breathing the air and waking up at noon all summer long. The lack of respect for our elders, community, and authority simply cannot be overlooked here. It is indeed an issue that leads to much larger problems as our youth gets older.

This is another area I cannot possibly stress enough that needs to be changed at its very core. We continuously reward our children with cell phones, laptops, flat screen TV's, and other gadgets without them having earned such things. Firstly, they do not need the cell phone until they get a job and a car. No exceptions, no asterisks because a parent is worried, etc. We got by just fine for two hundred years without this kind of luxury, and I have not seen one paragraph of data that shows our teens are smarter, better students, or safer with a cell phone. On the contrary, we have regressed in many key areas, so the phones have to go. The same goes for large screen TV's, cars, and other unnecessary toys. When your child throws a fit or tries to make you feel guilty because "Everybody else has one of these"—so what. When they apply this kind of pressure, they need to understand they are moving further and further away from getting what they want. Giving in by rewarding them with these luxurious toys is absolutely the worst thing we can do for teens and preteens. This very thing is at the center of why our children have no idea how to earn a buck when they graduate from high school. Most seventeen and eighteen-year-old boys and girls in America have no idea, not even a small clue, as to what the value of a US. dollar is. At the very least, even if your teen has been great throughout his or her middle- and high-school years, and he or she is carrying a 4.0 into his or her senior year, he or she still needs to pay for a portion of what he or she gets. Each child should work part time, earning enough to pay for gas and oil, minor repairs, and insurance at the very least. Purchasing an expensive automobile in our names and making the payments to the banks and insurance companies while giving even the best kid fifty dollars per week for gas is still a bad idea. They will never understand what it takes to own and care for something this way. We cannot continue to do everything for them. Waiting until seventeen to drive is not a bad idea either. Statistics clearly show sixteen-year-old drivers are too immature to operate a vehicle. Throw a cell phone into the mix, and we have a fatal situation waiting to happen.

This kind of thing is exactly what I see each and everyday in my own personal life. My stepdaughter just turned eighteen and is a senior in high school. Her grades are good and she is due to graduate on time. She also has aspirations to attend college next year. However, she also has a six-month-old daughter, who lives with us. My daughter is very immature, even for 18, and not ready for the world. She has never learned the hard lessons of life, the value of a dollar, etc. Her baby's biological father has no car, no money, no home, no steady job, and no income. His family's way of thinking is to put the cute little baby girl on government programs, collecting assistance for food and everything else. I have made it my personal mission to not let this happen. My daughter and her twenty-one-year-old "baby daddy" are simply not going to be handed anything. Not from myself or my wife, and not from the government. They are not just one, but two able-bodied young people who need to work and earn their keep. As much as my daughter needs a car, we have not purchased her one. While this imposes more wear and tear on my wife's automobile, and my daughter is still completely reliant on us for her transportation needs, giving her a car when she has no job and no way to pay for its basic upkeep is not the answer. We are making sacrifices to watch the baby girl while my daughter finishes school. My wife quit her teaching job to do this, and I fill in one or two days per week myself. My daughter will not be given a free ride, must get to work right after she graduates, and has been told time and time again to map out her future and game plans with and without her "baby daddy" in the picture. She has been told that a second pregnancy will not be tolerated, even if that means kicking her out on the street. And I will stick to that promise. The baby will get what she needs on my watch, and my step daughter will get love and encouragement from us. However, we will not allow either of them to be a burden on our taxpayers, and I expect the rest of us to start taking the same approach. It is necessary for our survival. If you make a mistake, no matter how young you are, it's not the end of the world, but you will have to pay for it with your own hard work, sweat and tears. Grandparents tend to get so enamored with the little bundles of joy that we find ourselves taking care of the baby for their irresponsible children. While it is wrong to withhold material and financial things from the baby, it is just as wrong for us to continue to enable our teens by giving them everything on a silver platter.

When we purchase things for our kids before they earn or deserve them, for no other reason than it may make things easier for us as parents, it sends the wrong signal. Kids and young adults need to understand how the system works, not how to get around it. Our horrible failure as parents in this area has been multiplied in a big way on Wall Street. We give children our children something for nothing without a plan to ever pay for it, and they learn nothing. Our banks loan money to people who cannot pay it back, and they learn nothing. It is all connected— trust me on that one. America must be disciplined, respectful, and well educated from this point forward. It needs to start in the home, at the age of four or five. *Creative parenting* and *creative accounting* are creative terms for laziness, shortcuts, and smoke and mirrors. Popping MAOIs and other pills are not a fix for most adults, so it should not even be considered for your ten year old. Shame on you if this is what you have done out of sheer laziness and self-centered parenting. That itself is what we need to understand fully, and we are not there right now. Being a good parent is a duty to our future, the community in which we live, and generations to come. Letting our kids go without love, discipline, structure, and the proper tools for success in the future is unacceptable. We can no longer fix things with a pill, a buyoff, or an unearned gift. Make them earn it, please, and they will thank you twenty years down the road. It may seem like too much hassle now, but it will pay off in the end.

Chapter 13
Our Best and Brightest

Since I am most definitely a "glass-half-full" kind of guy, and I believe we can indeed repair America at its core, I will choose not to look at things with complete gloom and doom. I could easily scare anyone who reads this into thinking the world is about to end, because we have failed so miserably on so many levels. After all, if these absolutely guilty-as-hell crooks and criminals behind the pyramid scams on Wall Street and the accounting scandals at Enron, Adelphia, Lehman Bros., WorldCom, Tyco, and others happen to be the cream of the crop, we are in deep trouble. If these guys were indeed the smartest, and earned their way to the top by being smart enough to wiz through MBA programs at Ivy League, Big Ten, and Pac Ten schools with flying colors, and they made these horrendously pathetic business decisions out of sheer stupidity, we may never recover. The other option is simple, but almost as scary when you think about it. If these clowns and klutzes like Bernie Ebbers, Ken Lay, and Dennis Kozloski (to name just a few) were just very clever criminals all along, lying and cheating their way to the top, we have a completely different issue to uncover and solve relatively quickly. We cannot afford any more messes like this.

Either way, bailing out the auto industry, Wall Street investment firms, and the banks with taxpayer money is essentially hocking our future to bail out the guys who were supposed to be our best and brightest – for both stupidity and greed-driven criminal activity. Did we miss something when these goofballs were in college? What are the warning signs to watch for in the future? I can tell you this for certain. We absolutely must do away with any and all seven- and eight-figure salaries, outrageous stock option clauses, and "golden parachute" multi-million-dollar deals right now! America's entire way of doing things and its collective way of thinking must be reversed. Yes, reverse it or start over from scratch. From this point forward, any business dealing in loans, investments, automobiles, money, and thousands and thousands of jobs—no matter what the product line may be—its business plan must be revamped and simplified. Paying people a ton of guaranteed funds in cash and stock makes no sense if you do so before they complete a single positive act. This kind of thing has never made sense to me. Even when I was a kid, I used to say, "Wait a minute, this guy drove the company stock and worth downward, but got a huge bonus. How can this be?" My father and grandfather would simply reply, "That is the way we do it in America, son." It made me sick then, and makes me nearly faint now. If the guy or gal at the very top of a corporation fails, they get nothing but a boot in the butt and a one-month severance pay deal. They should get stripped of their stock and perks, reprimanded by the board of directors, and fired. This is a much more common-sense way of doing things than letting corporate lawyers and bean counters tie things up for months or years while waiting for approval of golden parachute funds their client (a badly failed CEO) to be deposited into a Swiss numbered account. I've got news for you people on Wall Street: You belong in a cell right next to Bernie Ebbers and some of his buddies. Some of you are so crooked, so greedy, so evil, you may belong in the grave right next to Kenneth Lay. That is for a higher power to ultimately decide, but you can guess what my vote would be.

Where did we go wrong? How did we allow things like unrealistic credit lines, bad loans, unsecured debt and property, and terrible business plans to inflate the stock of these essentially worthless companies? Should we have seen it coming? If so, who should have seen it and put a stop to it? How the mighty have fallen and stabbed the world market in the back on the way down.

I simply do not understand. At what point in the past twenty-five or thirty years did we make it understood in the corporate world that real cash flow, real worth, a good product, and assets one could actually see and touch were not important? If you are falsely inflating the stock price and value of an essentially worthless company, is the stock not also worthless? Hello! Enron and its "brain trust" were masters at duping the stockholders, media, and their employees. What we need to fully understand as Americans is just how evil and greedy these folks had to be. Did they recruit these idiots at the Satanic Cult School of Business? The Tony Soprano, John Gotti, and Corleone family books were cleaner and more believable. If these guys were the best and brightest Houston had to offer, the nation's fourth-largest city is in serious despair. These bloodsuckers falsely inflated the stock and companies worth for years, all the while smiling and asking employees to sink their life savings into their worthless plan.

Here's a tip for those nitwits on Wall Street and such. The old saying "It takes money to make money" has been beaten, dragged thru the mud, and done to death. It appears financial institutions and investment firms have been living by this antiquated creed for too long. Who ever first uttered those infamous words most likely did not mean, "It takes a longer line of credit than can ever be paid back and several bad loans in the millions and billions to make money"—just a guess though. Is there a book that all these once-respected MBA programs carry that lays out these disastrous, fantasy-land-style business plans? If not, do these guys just play it by ear, getting the bankers so drunk they cannot read the fine print and will just sign any ridiculous thing? It seems pretty clear to me that even a first-year student in a local community college Business 101 course would know better than borrowing or loaning more money than can realistically ever be paid back to the lender. Perhaps we should have viewed the tragic happenings of September 11, 2001,

just a bit more closely. Sure, it was just a few wacked out, delusional, living-in-the-stone-ages, moronic Muslims getting their jollies by ending their miserable lives while taking thousands of innocent civilians with them. They caught America with her pants down for sure, but we may need to look at the photos and images caught just after the 9/11 attacks and view them as much more than a Muslim-verses-the-West terrorist thing. Perhaps this event was a forecast of what was happening already on Wall Street and in the American financial sector. The images of the World Trade Center reduced to a pile of rubble and bodies still haunts us today, and will do so for another hundred years or more. But the fact that the World Trade Center and Pentagon were targeted by these crazed murders should not be viewed as mere attention getters and eye openers for those who carried the plan out. Those two buildings, along with the White House, are perhaps the truest symbols of corruption and failure over the past thirty to fifty years that we have on Earth. Did the clerk on the eighty-fourth floor deserve to die at the hands of a confused nut? No way. Still, the World Trade Center was a mighty symbol of power, greed, and capitalism. The images of its destruction and rubble after the event are still hauntingly clear to me, as if this is what our country had left itself vulnerable to then, and for many years to come.

I am not certain just how deep the cover up goes, but I can guarantee someone dropped the ball on the 9/11 terrorist attacks. Nobody will be able to convince me that Mohammed Attah and his retarded cronies were not on some sort of watch list at the Pentagon or CIA Headquarters in Langley, Virginia. If this is true, and I know it is, how is it Attah and the others were allowed to sit around the airport, looking pissed off because they have had neither a shower nor a woman in weeks? Somebody was asleep at the wheel, and it was probably someone pretty high up the security clearance and pay grades. It is time to forget about racial and religious profiling backlash. I say execute a full-body cavity search on each and every one of those robe-wearing, face-hiding travelers at all airports. Hurting someone's feelings is a much better idea than allowing them to possibly bring down an aircraft with two hundred and fifty people onboard. At least we appear to have been getting that part right over the past few years.

Our best and brightest are currently serving in Afghanistan and Iraq as well as other places around the world. Some of them should be given an opportunity to run things in the financial sector when they return. They cannot possibly do any worse than the MBA's and bean counters have been doing. We now can clearly see what the few hundred powerful men and women with complete control of the world markets have been driven by all these years: greed. Yes, nothing more than bloody greed. They have not applied good business sense or common sense, or checked the pulse of the average consumer; that's for certain. These same greedy bastards have also come up with zero in the way of a contingency plan when the markets collapse. So, in a nutshell, these few hundred people in the five-hundred-million to several-billion net worth range have only accomplished extreme wealth for themselves, at the mere cost of the American economy, global stability, and our once proud and solid reputation. Nice work, guys! Hanging in the town square is too good for the people on this list who saw this coming but purposely did nothing to stop it. After all, when it is all said and done, and the markets come back, they will likely get even richer. Our best and brightest financial and business minds have done the world a great disservice. It would certainly appear these people are only best at lining their own pockets and then scurrying under the couch when the lights come on as things go badly.

The best and brightest minds are at the helm in Motown, too. How far did they think union contracts that made sense thirty years ago would take them in a current global marketplace?

How far did they think outrageous bonus checks, 95 percent pay for no work, and the best health care in the nation would last while losing money hand-over-fist for many years?

Yes, hindsight is indeed twenty-twenty, but the current UAW contracts, operating costs, and salary and hourly-wage structures have been unrealistic for more than fifteen years. I grew up in Detroit and I can tell you first-hand that many of my friends and acquaintances bragged for years about their bonuses and fat paychecks during shut-down periods. Yes, the UAW managed to sucker management at the Big Three into paying all their workers a ton of money even when they were not making cars. GM sells the same number of cars as Toyota sells in each of the past several years, but one company makes nine to eleven billion, the other loses at least that much. Those kinds of numbers did not happen overnight. The powers that be at GM, Ford, and Chrysler certainly did not wake up ten days before they went to Capital Hill for a handout and say, "Man, we were making money like crazy two months ago, what the heck happened?" That is for sure. When your company is losing hundreds or millions of dollars each month, flying private jets around the country, collecting fat bonus checks, and conducting business the same way it did when things were going well, it makes about as much sense as giving a ex-convict TV preacher from Louisiana your entire life savings. I still cannot believe the ladies and gents sitting in the board rooms in Troy, Dearborn, and downtown Detroit have been signing off on this crap for the past ten to fifteen years. It boggles the mind.

From this point forward, we need to use our brains better than we have been doing. Signing off on a business plan or contract that you know will not work, but doing so just to keep the doors open can no longer be a viable option. We can no longer trust someone completely just because he or she went to a prestigious university for six to eight years. Experience, common sense, and a solid strategy for growth are the only things that make sense. I am sorry, but if we have to let the Big Three automakers be gutted and completely restructured, then so be it. Bonuses, fat salaries, some health care benefits, and a percentage of hourly wages are going to have to be cut, no doubt about it. I do not think it's fair at all to take anything away from the former hard-working retirees, as many of them were directly responsible for making the Big Three great. These guys and gals worked there when the car companies actually turned a profit. The reality is that drastic measures have to be taken in Detroit, on Wall Street, and across the banking and mortgage industries. Not next quarter, next year, or fifteen months from now. This needs to happen right now, at the start of the year 2009.

Chapter 14
The How, Why, and When

Each and every company with direct effect on the American economic environment needs to act right now. This cannot wait. I can tell you what the first step needs to be without hesitation. You draw up binding contracts with very real consequences, perhaps much more than financial ones. You hand said contracts to the people in charge at each and every company losing money, and they either sign it or they don't. If they do not sign it, they are out, so bring on the next leader. Bring in people who want to go down with the ship when she sinks. Bring in people who fully understand when you sit them down face-to-face and tell them the company is literally in their hands. Ask, "Do you want this responsibility?" If they fail, they lose everything. No more twenty-million-dollar golden parachutes on the way to the next easy gig. The language within these new corporate leadership contracts needs to be straight, to the point, and very clearly explained. This can be done in twenty pages, not in two thousand pages of legal jargon intended to confuse everyone. You lay out a realistic, yet competitive base salary, and the same health care and paid vacation and holidays as the rest of the people under them. Only if and when the company hits certain, hard-line business goals and financial watermarks does he or she on the top floor get incentive or bonus pay. If things go from bad to worse, you are out on the street, no questions or legal avenues available. You get four to six weeks severance (base) pay just like the rest of us. This newly signed boss would not become filthy rich, gain more operational control, and be anointed back to "fat cat" status until the company does well for eight consecutive quarters. If and when these eight quarters come, the board and employees can vote on what percentage of stock and cash rewards they see fit for their new hero. You fail. You not only *do not* collect a fat reward; you are out immediately, relinquishing all stock options at the current market rate, minus 15 percent to 20 percent, depending on the agreement. Yes, that is right; you'll lose your job and pay. Stock fine for allowing the stock to go down on your watch. Nothing else matters. You'll get people driven by success and a real fear of failure to sign this kind of a deal. The flip-floppers, self-centered, protect-myself-at-all-costs, damn-the-company-and-its-employees-types will never go for this. Fine, that is just what we want and need. Don't let the door hit you in the rear end on the way out, sir.

I apologize for taking a shot at the hourly workers in Motown as well, but it needs to be taken. Sorry, folks; but twenty-five to twenty-nine dollars per hour, straight out of high school with full benefits is no longer doable. These folks may work hard, but they will have to be onboard with the company for at least five years before they become comfortable. I have been in IT since 1987, and I started on the very bottom. Like many others in my field, it took fifteen years to make anywhere close to seventy-five thousand dollars per year, and twenty years to start knocking down anything close to six figures. Keep in mind, we are working for profitable companies, getting top-notch reviews each year, good attendance, etc. The UAW and similar organizations mean well, but guaranteed money at a high rate for a nonproductive or out-on-sick-leave employee makes no sense. These new hires need to be started at a more reasonable sixteen dollars per hour, and given reduced rates on health care insurance, perhaps splitting 60/40 with the company, only after completing the six-month probationary period. There will be *no overtime.* You make your hourly rate; that's it. Benefits kickin after six months of hard work and good attendance. Paying a billion dollars a year in overtime makes no sense when a company is losing money. The ability for low and mid-level managers and supervisors to approve overtime must be stripped completely.

Times are tough for the automakers right now. That means a competent white-collar person will have to oversee two or three departments in the foreseeable future. Large, very real cuts and sacrifices have to be made right now for survival in the auto industry. It is truly do or die.

Where to start with this mess in the banking, investment, and mortgage areas? I think the same types of contracts and terms for the people at the top of the money-shuffling industry can be applied. The incoming CEOs, COOs, presidents, and high-ranking flunkies who report to those folks will have to understand that business as we have known it for many years is no longer status quo. What has "worked" in the past did not really work, so doing things in as opposite a fashion as one can would probably be a good idea. Investment firms and banks these days simply move funds around electronically, trying to hide losses in order to inflate the stock, etc. Now that we all now and understand that fact, these people at the top will be under a high-powered microscope. They simply will not be able to float loans to large or small businesses, high-profile investors, and other banks if there is a good chance the loan terms cannot be met. This goes way deeper than a credit score. We will have to dig much deeper into the background and history of the people and groups to whom you are loaning money. No information will be sacred in the future. Say you have a real chunk of money sitting in a vault—say ten billion dollars. That money must be considered everything for your lending institution from this point forward. You approve the sending out of those funds, they have to come back—each and every one of those dollars, plus interest, or you fail and close up shop. Comprende?

A very good second step would be to outlaw anything even remotely resembling a "Ponzi" or pyramid scam. The crooks who orchestrated these schemes over the past twenty-five years or more should be shot in Times Square at high noon. These people in the money-shuffling world will tell you that what I am proposing is not realistic or feasible in the eyes of the board of directors, etc. Tough, it has to be feasible. Sign on the dotted line,

Mr. Smith, and get the job done right, or you will be fired, replaced, and maybe even prosecuted. Playing dumb like we did not know any better cannot be accepted by the American public any longer. If a highly paid, highly educated, highly experienced CEO or boss claims he or she did not know what was happening right under his or her nose, we must know with 100 percent certainty he or she is lying through their teeth. This is the way we will have to approach business from this point forward. The people in the past and present who have made the decisions, signed the documents, loans, and checks have quite frankly failed miserably. That means that no matter how smart, loyal, trustworthy, and good with numbers the next few generations of leaders may be...and no matter how sincere their intentions may be from deep down in their guts, they will not be trusted. That is where sheer greed has gotten us.

As I have stated many times in the previous chapters and paragraphs, we must ac t now. We must act with an iron fist. Since we cannot completely trust the lawyers, politicians, bean counters, and MBA types sitting in the big offices anymore, you and I will have to find a way to implement our own checks and balances. Perhaps we can come up with an electronic-fence-type dog collar for humans? Well, maybe not that, but we need something along those lines. Our way of thinking has to quickly morph into an automatic reflex and overall mindset that each and every dollar is important. Moreover, let's see to it that these dollars are real and not lines of credit.

For the United States of America to regain its prestigious position at the top of the global business, financial, and investing food chains, we have to become humble overnight. We simply must admit that we are not nearly as good as we lead the rest of the world to believe. Our way of doing things on many levels is broken, antiquated, and downright wrong. With that being said, we need to swallow a little pride and see how others are competing against the likes of Germany, the US, and China. Our culture has taught our business leaders to spend huge to get a little in return, and this just does not work. Spending money to make money on things like initial startup costs, advertising, and essential workforce personnel makes good business sense. Using every dime of a seven-billion-dollar line of credit just for the heck of it, without a prayer in hell of ever being able to pay this money back, makes no sense, even in the crazy, crooked world of Wall Street. America cannot afford to get the next five to ten years wrong. We have to be accountable to ourselves in every way, shape, and form of which we can think. We must beg for the rest of the world's forgiveness, and hope like heck they can do business with us with confidence somewhere in the not-too-distant future.

I love this country. I wish there were more positive things I could say about our political and business world leaders, but there just is not much there. Let us be strong together over the next ten to fifty years, and maybe we can once again thrive.

Epilogue

It will be difficult for us as a nation to apply commonsense, with our leaders not applying it. However, we must go forward and take matters into our own hands on a local level first, repairing our homes, communities, and cities. The political monster in Washington, DC, has gotten so out of control, it may take a complete disaster for those clowns to see the light. That may indeed be the only way they will remove their self-serving, fantasy-world blinders. Our current president seems to think larger government, more spending, printing more money, and worrying about the bill later is the way to go. Our children, their children, and their children will have to foot the bill. Not fair and not smart on any level of thinking. During the Ronald Reagan presidency, less government jobs and spending—along with a smaller, simplified IRS and tax code— actually worked. The US government made more during this time than in the previous few years. In several other countries, less governing, more common sense, a simplified tax code, and an overall responsible way of letting the people run their own country has worked for a few hundred years. The number-one of America has become itself, but others will soon follow and become a very real threat if we do not wake up and repair some things now. The two-party system is broken, and most educated people without an underlying self-serving political agenda can easily see it. The Libertarian way of thinking about flat-tax proposals may only have a 5% following at this juncture in time. However, these things may be born out of necessity in just a few years.